AT HIS FEET

AT HIS FEET

Drawing Closer to Christ with the Women of the New Testament

DERYA LITTLE

Our Sunday Visitor
Huntington, Indiana

Nihil Obstat
Msgr. Michael Heintz, Ph.D.
Censor Librorum

Imprimatur
✠ Kevin C. Rhoades
Bishop of Fort Wayne-South Bend
November 11, 2020

Except where noted, the Scripture citations used in this work are taken from the *Revised Standard Version of the Bible — Second Catholic Edition* (Ignatius Edition), copyright © 1965, 1966, 2006 National Council of the Churches of Christ in the United States of America. Used by permission. All rights reserved.

Every reasonable effort has been made to determine copyright holders of excerpted materials and to secure permissions as needed. If any copyrighted materials have been inadvertently used in this work without proper credit being given in one form or another, please notify Our Sunday Visitor in writing so that future printings of this work may be corrected accordingly.

Copyright © 2021 by Derya Little
29 28 27 26 25   3 4 5 6 7 8 9

All rights reserved. With the exception of short excerpts for critical reviews, no part of this work may be reproduced or transmitted in any form or by any means whatsoever without permission from the publisher. For more information, visit: www.osv.com/permissions.

Our Sunday Visitor Publishing Division
Our Sunday Visitor, Inc.
200 Noll Plaza
Huntington, IN 46750
www.osv.com
1-800-348-2440

ISBN: 978-1-68192-590-5 (Inventory No. T2456)
1. RELIGION—Biblical Studies—Bible Study Guides.
2. RELIGION—Christian Life—Women's Issues.
3. RELIGION—Christianity—Catholic.

eISBN: 978-1-68192-591-2
LCCN: 2020949678

Cover and interior design: Amanda Falk
Cover art: AdobeStock

PRINTED IN THE UNITED STATES OF AMERICA

Dedicated to
Our Lady, Star of the Sea

Contents

Introduction 9

1. Saint Elizabeth: What is your guilt? 13

2. Saint Anna the Prophetess:
   Can you be content with a simple life? 23

3. Peter's Mother-in-Law: Can you face your selfishness? ... 31

4. Saint Photine: Who do you want to be? 39

5. The Bleeding Woman: Do you meet God in prayer? ... 49

6. Justa: Where did God find you? 57

7. Saint Mary Magdalene: What lies do you believe? ... 67

8. Saint Martha: Can you handle the mundane? 75

9. Saint Joanna: Can you serve without recognition? ... 85

10. Saint Priscilla: Are you willing to be a co-missionary? ... 95

11. Saint Lydia of Thyatira: What will you do with his gift? ... 105

12. Our Lady: How can you keep the fire alive? 113

Epilogue 123

Introduction

"Trust God that you are where you are meant to be," said the great Doctor of the Church Saint Teresa of Ávila. Some of us have traveled long distances to arrive at our destination, and some have traveled but a little. Yet, wherever we are, the journey to becoming a saint is not always easy, and sometimes it is hard to find a fellow traveler.

At least that was the case for me, since the Lord found me in a land that is spiritually far from his Church. I was raised in a Muslim household. My parents' divorce led me to read the life of Muhammad and the Quran more closely, instead of simply trusting my parents. My distrust of them had turned into distrust of everything they taught me, including being a Muslim. When I became an atheist at a young age, I embraced a chain-free life, in which the only god I worshipped was myself. Lacking a reliable family and any moral compass made me hard-hearted and depraved. A sinful life was all that was available to me until, at the age of nineteen, I met a Christian for the first time. For years, she and I argued about God's existence and the historicity of Jesus. Despite being annoyed and frustrated that I could not refute this Christian's claims, I went back for more, because that was where Truth had led me. When I was baptized a few years later, the Lord had opened a door that would lead to a lifetime of adventure and unexpected joy.

As I learned about my new faith and devoured all the Christian books I could get my hands on in Turkey, questions about being a Protestant popped into my head. I carefully pushed them aside until a good friend decided to join the "papist cult." Suddenly I realized I was finding answers to my questions about Protestantism and its teachings within virtual and actual pages of Catholic books. When I was received into the Catholic Church in 2008, I found myself in uncharted waters, where being a Catholic woman remained an enigma.

In the middle of this desert, the women of the New Testament gave me inspiration and guidance. Their stories in the Holy Scriptures gave me glimpses into what it means to live a life of love, faith, and hope in the Barque of Peter. After all, regardless of how much time has passed between our lives and theirs, human nature, concupiscence, and sin remain afflictions in our lives. The remedy and the source of our salvation also remain the same. Even though our lives may look considerably different from the lives of women in first-century Israel, their heartaches, struggles, worries, and their remedies still resonate through the ages.

We must trust the wisdom of the Holy Spirit in choosing these women and their stories out of countless others, and must pay attention to the lessons they can teach us in our journey to sainthood. In this book, you will find the stories of twelve women of the New Testament. The names of most of these women are recorded in the Bible, but some names are lost to history.

Regardless, they all encountered Our Lord in a special way that changed the courses of their lives.

The corresponding Scripture verses are noted at the beginning of each chapter for your reflection and prayer. I encourage you to keep your Bible close by and to read the Scripture first, whether you are reading this book alone or in a study group. Each chapter begins with a short glance into the life of the woman, to bring you back in time and allow you to walk in her shoes. Then I share how her example affected my life. I hope that, in reading my story, you will also see how these women's examples can apply to your own life and circumstances. Each chapter ends with a few reflection questions for personal use or for group study.

As Saint Teresa said, first we need to trust God with our lives and know that we are not alone in this journey, even in the darkest hour. My hope is that, in reading this book, you will find that you are not alone in your journey as a Christian woman. Together with the women of the New Testament, we will learn to seek Jesus, who seeks us first, and to sit at his feet as his disciples and daughters.

My prayers are with you as you seek his goodness and mercy in the lives of these blessed women.

1

Saint Elizabeth

WHAT IS YOUR GUILT?

Read Luke 1:5-80

As a Levite, a priest of the Most Holy Lord, Zechariah was accustomed to life in the Jewish temple. But entering the Holy of Holies, where the Alpha and the Omega came down, was different. His heart started to pound in his chest. One of the other priests had tied a thick rope around his ankle, a reminder that he would be alone, just like Moses on Mount Zion. The silence that surrounded the preparation added to Zechariah's anxiety. This was no simple affair. If something awful happened to him while he was in the most sacred part of the Temple, the other priests would pull him out using this rope, for no one else was allowed to enter. Yet, even with the solemnity of the moment, nothing could have prepared him for the news he was about to receive.

The angel Gabriel appeared in all his heavenly majesty. Zechariah froze in his place, his heart threatening to jump out of his chest. Sweat ran down his back. He was glad to have that rope around his ankle. God's holy messenger announced that he and his wife, Elizabeth, would have a son after years of being barren. "How could that be?" Zechariah thought. "We are old, too old, to bring new life to the world." They had gotten used to the emptiness and silence of their house, as the houses of their neighbors teemed with life and laughter.

Zechariah did not — or could not — believe the angel Gabriel. And the messenger of the Lord does not take kindly to those who doubt his words, as Luke records:

> I am Gabriel, who stand in the presence of God; and I was sent to speak to you, and to bring you this good news. And behold, you will be silent and unable to speak until the day that these things come to pass, because you did not believe my words, which will be fulfilled in their time. (Luke 1:19–20)

It is safe to assume that Zechariah found a way to explain to Elizabeth all that happened in the Holy of Holies, and Elizabeth, at the sight of her mute husband, probably knew better than to doubt Gabriel's words.

Even today, many women feel ashamed and inadequate when they cannot conceive. That feeling of shame was much more intense in the first century than in our own age. Today a woman's worth is so often based on how much money she makes or how expensive her shoes are.

We can only assume that Elizabeth had prayed in the darkness, offered sacrifices in the Temple, and begged in the daylight for a son who would become a priest like his father, who would carry on the name, or for a daughter who would take care of her and Zechariah and bring joy to her mother's barren life. For decades, she prayed, and no answer came.

By the time Gabriel taught a lesson in obedience and humility to Zechariah, all hope seemed lost for Elizabeth, as month after month passed without a sign of fertility. According to the cultural norms of her day (as still happens in many Eastern cultures), she was shunned for being less than whole. Her womanhood was not complete because she could not have children. Day by day, her prayers went unheeded and her shame doubled; quadrupled. The women at the well smiled and nodded to her face because her husband was a priest, but smiles turned into whispers as soon as she walked away. Women her age enjoyed the respect and company of grandchildren along with the help and doting of daughters and sons. But only a quiet house waited for Elizabeth, and only two people to cook and clean for. Her wisdom went unshared. Tiny baby clothes went unworn.

That is, until her husband came home unable to talk after he had been chosen by lot to enter the Holy of Holies. Maybe Zechariah found a piece of chalk and a board to tell her about his incredible encounter with the Lord's messenger. Elizabeth hoped against hope as the scratching of chalk on board shared the best news she had heard for a long time. Could it be true? Could her womb, which was past its childbearing days, produce a joyful fruit? Could it be that one day she could walk to the well with her toddler at her heels, holding on to her skirts?

> After these days his wife Elizabeth conceived, and for five months she hid herself, saying, "Thus the Lord has

done to me in the days when he looked on me, to take away my reproach among men." (Luke 1:24–25)

Elizabeth loved the Lord even though her prayers for a child went unheard. More than likely, she would have continued to live a saintly life, albeit unrecorded, had she not conceived John the Baptist at the word of Gabriel. She had learned to deal with the shame and to live an unremarkable life as the other women around her enjoyed the fruits of their wombs. However, that was not her fate. When she became pregnant at an old age, she was humbled that the Lord of the universe would bestow such a wonderful gift on her.

After hearing Gabriel's joyful news, Elizabeth had a bounce in her step, and her shoulders did not carry the burden of a life lived in the shadow of her neighbors' judgment. She smiled much more easily and enjoyed the sound of young ones. The Lord had taken her shame away, and she was breathless for it, lest she should wake up from a dream.

Pregnancy was not the only blessing God would give Elizabeth:

> In those days Mary arose and went with haste into the hill country, to a city of Judah, and she entered the house of Zechariah and greeted Elizabeth. And when Elizabeth heard the greeting of Mary, the child leaped in her womb; and Elizabeth was filled with the Holy Spirit and she exclaimed with a loud cry, "Blessed are you among women, and blessed is the fruit of your womb! And why is this granted me, that the mother of my Lord should come to me? For behold, when the voice of your greeting came to my ears, the child in my womb leaped for joy. And blessed is she who believed that there would be a fulfillment of what was spoken to her from the

Lord." (Luke 1:39–45)

Not only had Elizabeth been blessed with a baby of her own, but the Immaculate Conception visited her while the Word of God slowly grew in her womb. The Lord took her shame away and brought the salvation of mankind to her humble home. The meeting of Elizabeth and Mary was so momentous that it became one of the joyful mysteries of the Holy Rosary.

Since the moment Eve believed the serpent's lie in the Garden of Eden, her daughters have shared her fate in falling for his deceptions. We hear his lies over and over in our heads. Without the grace of God, our sinful nature prompts us to sin, and once we fall, the accuser always reminds us that we have fallen, insinuating that we are not worthy of God's love, that we should burn and die under the burden of our unforgivable sin. Surely Elizabeth heard these lies year after year, as her womb remained empty. This was her guilt, until the Lord set her free.

• • •

Elizabeth's infertility was no fault of her own. The infertility I struggled with for years, however, was of my own making. Without any understanding of life or sin, and with the selfishness of a teenage girl who was not willing to accept the consequences of her actions, I found myself sitting in front of a gynecologist with my boyfriend. Since Islam does not have a universal teaching on when life begins, abortion is a somewhat murky issue. Some Muslims believe it is always sinful to end a pregnancy, and some believe it is acceptable until the day the soul enters the body, at the time of quickening. In Turkey, abortion is legal until twenty weeks and is performed by doctors who also deliver babies.

When I speak and write about my abortions, I am often told that my account is sterile, almost devoid of emotions. When I look back to those painful days and what followed them, sterile is the perfect description of how I felt. Sterile means incapable of producing offspring, barren and free from living organisms. As my boyfriend and I sat with the doctor, who wore an eerie smile befitting someone who was about to take a life, I felt as if someone else was in charge of my body and I was simply a spectator. As an atheist, of course, my intellect had come up with many justifications for what was about to happen. But something was amiss; my smothered conscience was trying to get my attention, but years of decadence and indifference had made me incapable of hearing it. It was remarkable how much sin had clouded my intellect. But in the sterile environment of that doctor's office, my heart and soul had become barren as well.

Unlike the accounts of seedy abortion clinics that make it into the headlines, this office was well kept. The doctor cared about the hygiene of his workplace and even for my well-being. The hundred dollars we had to procure for the abortion, I could tell, was not his only concern. He tried to reassure me that I would be safe, that it was a simple "procedure," that I would not even remember it had happened, and that it would be painless. I nodded absentmindedly as he strung words together to make me feel better, but there were no feelings inside me to heed his words. I just wanted it to be over.

He was right: It was physically painless, other than the two weeks of bleeding that followed. But he was wrong to say that soon that day would become a distant memory. Oh, how little did we know about the cost of taking innocent lives! And this would not be my last abortion.

Looking back, I don't know how culpable I was in making the decision to abort. I lived in a country where teenage pregnancies were unheard of. I had no financial or emotional support. The men I was with would not even consider having a baby at that stage of their lives, even if I wanted to. So it was not only my atheism that pushed me but also my circumstances. I am trying not to absolve myself of wrongdoing, but to explain that, despite the level of my culpability and my lack of belief in the existence of a soul, those abortions left a deep scar. Despite everything, I heard that tiny voice buried deep inside my head, but I refused to listen. When I finally heeded the voice of conscience years later, the love and forgiveness I received was indescribable. For all those years, the Lord had pursued me, regardless of my unfaithfulness.

Still, for a long time, I could not talk about the abortions. The very first time I told anyone was when Therese, the missionary who shared the Good News of Christ with me for the first time, took me to a lady who prayed for those with complicated backgrounds like mine. Finally, that festering secret was out in the open. Even though Therese was there, it was easier for me to talk about it to a stranger. Both women cried with me and prayed for me. What was most memorable was Therese's prayer that my womb would be open to life again.

That day and many days after that, Therese prayed for me. But the shame of my actions never quite left me. I could not let go. I could not forgive myself, despite being baptized in the name of the Holy Trinity. In my shame, I found an unlikely friend in the pages of the New Testament: Saint Elizabeth, mother of Saint John the Baptist, who would one day baptize his cousin Jesus.

The Lord knows us, and he knows our desire to hear his healing words. Years after my baptism, I found myself waiting in line for my first confession, because in a few days I would be received into the Catholic Church. I did not want to be there. I did not want to talk about my past or present sins. But there is a reason Christ has asked us to confess our sins, not just to God but to each other. When the gentle priest asked me over and over why I was there, all I could say was, "I killed my own children."

Then the priest, whom I had never seen before and will probably never see again, said the words of absolution: "God, the Father of mercies, through the death and resurrection of his Son has reconciled the world to himself and sent the Holy Spirit among us for the forgiveness of sins; through the ministry of the Church may God give you pardon and peace, and I absolve you from your sins in the name of the Father, and of the Son, and of the Holy Spirit." My *amen* came drowned in a stream of tears, because in that priest's voice, I heard Christ himself, as if he held my hand and wiped away my tears. What I had known in my head finally reached down to my heart to erase my shame forever.

Of course, I still think about the babies — how old they would have been or whether they had brown eyes. The regret will never leave me, but they have forgiven me, just as Christ has. I ask them to pray for their mommy, their daddies, and their siblings. I hope and pray that I meet them in heaven one day and see for myself whether they have brown eyes like me.

• • •

That unbearable shame is where Elizabeth finds us, regardless of the source of that shame, which the father of lies uses to accuse us in the darkness of the night. Where do your thoughts and heart wander when all else falls quiet? Each of us has a little secluded room in our mind where we do not let the Lord approach — where we hide our shame. What is hidden in yours?

If we are guiltless, as Elizabeth was in her infertility, she will be a friend who listens and gives a helping hand. If we suffer from the shame of sin, which is fitting in order to bring us to repentance, Saint Elizabeth will always be there to remind us to thank God, because she knew that it was the Lord who lifted her shame among men.

Saint Elizabeth, pray for us.

QUESTIONS FOR REFLECTION

What do you appreciate most about the way Elizabeth handled her cross?

What does Elizabeth's barrenness remind you of in your life?

What guilt or shame do you carry around needlessly? How can Elizabeth's example help you relinquish that guilt and live in the fullness of God's love?

2

Saint Anna the Prophetess

CAN YOU BE CONTENT WITH A SIMPLE LIFE?

Read Luke 2:36–38

The temple of the Lord always bustled with people, especially the spacious Court of the Gentiles, where all were welcome to the house of the Lord. The sunlight bounced off the light-colored rock pavement, making the noon sun even brighter. Still, people from all around the world came to visit the Temple and perhaps say a prayer. This was the place where curiosity and devotion melted into a sea of crowds.

Fifteen stairs led to the first part of the temple proper, each one of these steps forming a massive rectangle, surrounding the inner courts, which were not open to the gentiles. Only Jews were allowed beyond the steps.

In the daily hustle and bustle of Jews and gentiles at the Temple, a quiet old woman with soft steps and gentle manner did not stand out. Anna usually spent her days in prayer and fasting. Her work was prayer, and her prayer was work. She couldn't tell where one ended and the other began.

She rested her weary body on those monumental steps as she talked to complete strangers about the Lord, guiding lost souls back to the herd. The work of the Lord never ended, and there was always someone who needed to hear his voice. Anna was happy to deliver his words to those who were willing to listen:

> And there was a prophetess, Anna, the daughter of Phanuel, of the tribe of Asher; she was of a great age, having lived with her husband seven years from her virginity, and as a widow till she was eighty-four. She did not depart from the Temple, worshiping with fasting and prayer night and day. And coming up at that very hour she gave thanks to God, and spoke of him to all who were looking for the redemption of Jerusalem. (Luke 2:36–38)

Anna's father's name was Phanuel, which means "face of God." His daughter would see the face of God in the Temple, which had been built generations ago to make sure that only Levites would be able to enter the Holy of Holies, where Yahweh dwelt. On the steps that led up to the place where no man could go, Anna saw the face of God in a tiny baby.

The encounter in which she recognized Jesus is the central theme of her story, but she had to wait a long time to get there. Saint Luke records that she was married for only seven years before her husband died. Although it is uncertain when she married (some traditions say she was fourteen), Anna was likely widowed in her twenties. Even though Jewish law allowed her to marry again, Anna chose to stay single. The Gospel tells us that she was eighty-four when she met the Holy Family. This means that she likely waited in the Temple for six decades before she saw Jesus. She waited and waited, year after year, at the temple of the Lord. We do not even know whether she knew what she was waiting for. Perhaps she just chose to live a simple and quiet life in the presence of the Lord among those who sought him.

Since the New Testament is not known for wasting words, I wonder why Saint Luke mentions her age. After all, he does not tell us the ages of Saint Joseph, Simeon, or even Our Lady. Why was Anna singled out? I think Saint Luke wants to make clear how long this faithful woman had to wait to see the face of God.

Just before she laid eyes on Baby Jesus, she may have heard Simeon's proclamation that this child was the long-awaited Messiah: "Behold, this child is set for the fall and rising of many in Israel, and for a sign that is spoken against (and a sword will pierce through your own soul also), that thoughts out of many hearts may be revealed" (Lk 2:34–35).

As was her custom, Anna was at the Temple praying. It was like any other day, with people going in and out, offering sacrifices and prayers. Maybe she did not think much of it when this small family appeared with their infant, all swaddled, his face barely visible under the wraps. Maybe she recognized that something was different about the mother or that the father looked as if he carried an immense responsibility. Then Anna heard Simeon's proclamation and knew that that tiny babe was what she had been expecting (whether she realized it or not) for sixty years. With inexpressible joy, she approached Mary and Joseph because she knew who Christ was. It was a moment of recognition or supernatural intuition.

For decades, Anna had told people about Yahweh, the Creator of the universe, and his unending patience with Israel. As a woman of prayer, she lived her life in the Temple in utter simplicity, hoping only to gain the eternal treasure. But when she met Emmanuel and held him in her fragile old arms, she recognized that the prophetic light of the Old Testament focused on Christ, through whom salvation would come to pass. Because she was a prophetess, she also recognized other souls who were looking for the face of God. To these searching souls, Anna talked only about the salvation of Jerusalem and the one who would destroy and raise the very temple in which she spent her life. From that day on, she probably spoke only about Jesus as the fulfillment of all other prophecies.

We know very little about Saint Anna the prophetess, aside from what a few verses in Luke's Gospel tell us, but she was one of the few blessed ones who recognized the Christ Child well before his ministry started. Her persistent life of prayer and fasting allowed her to recognize the face of God in the middle of the daily crowd and to spread his good news even before he himself was able to talk.

The world around her was loud and busy and always offered distraction, but in the midst of the noise, she was able to claim silence for her soul so that the voice of the Father could penetrate the clamor of life. The priests, teachers, and sellers in the Temple were part of the same cacophony and busyness. The strong current of their daily lives drowned out the whisper of their Lord, who never forces himself into our souls. How many people saw the Holy Family that day but did not hear the gentle nudging that would have allowed them to see the face of the Christ Child? How many of them had their minds and souls cluttered with the never-ending worries of the world? Yet Anna's heart was calm when Mary and Joseph approached with their infant, and the whisper was loud enough to hear.

Now she is enjoying his presence in heaven, interceding for clueless souls who mistake simplicity for dullness and silence for boredom.

∴

If I had been a Jewish woman in the first century, living in Jerusalem and visiting the Temple frequently, I might have thought the life of Anna the prophetess was boring and tedious. Every day and night, she prayed and fasted, talked to people she might never see again, and did menial work. This was her life, as year after year passed while she became more and more fragile.

But there is much to be learned from silence. For a long time, I did not appreciate the beauty of a humble life devoid of recognition and success. Anna the prophetess made the choice to live simply, but simplicity came to me unexpectedly.

I know I would think Anna's life dreary, because that is what I thought about the sleepy coal town that marriage threw me into. Surrounded by thick woods, this village was listless and uninteresting. There was nothing to do and nowhere to go. Unlike Anna, I was not wise enough to see the holiness that could come out of a life of simplicity and silence. Little did I know that the Lord had given me an amazing gift by plucking me out of my complex and noisy city life and replanting me in a rural town where I could see not only the stars, but also — if I was willing — his face.

In his book *The Power of Silence*, Cardinal Robert Sarah speaks about the consequences of noise in our heads and hearts: "Without silence, God disappears in the noise. And this noise becomes all the more obsessive because God is absent. Unless the world rediscovers silence, it is lost. The earth then rushes into nothingness." In order to recognize that my soul was drowning in a sea of sometimes external and often internal noises, first I needed to learn what it meant to be in literal silence.

For many years after I left my hometown of Eregli at the age of eighteen (a town that would be considered sizable with its population of fifty thousand), big cities were my home: Istanbul, Ankara, and Newcastle. Then I met the love of my life and moved to a small town to marry him. The tiny coal town, built a century ago to accommodate the miners who worked nearby, is far off the beaten path. After exiting the interstate, you drive along narrow back roads that twist and turn under tall trees. A small waterfall spills over brown rocks and disappears into a creek that runs under the winding country road. It is one of the most scenic routes I have ever taken. My mother, who visited us a few years later, was so scared of the dark and ominous woods that every time we drove to the nearby town for shopping, she would pray all the way there and back.

My first few months in the small town were slow as my fiancé and I waited for our wedding in Turkey. During the day, I cleaned the house that would become our home very soon. Since I did not have a driver's license yet, I could leave only when my fiancé took me out. Until I moved to this public-transportation-free town, I could go wherever I wanted. Now, in the most advanced and wealthiest country in the world, I was trapped in a house with a bunch of brown furniture, waiting to be walked like a puppy dog. That loss of independence and self-reliance was at first very hard for me, even though the housework and my dissertation gave me something to do.

To be honest, the simplicity of life in a small town took me unawares. Until the move, having found the love of my life and the prospect of getting married had occupied my thoughts so densely that I did not even consider the massive changes in my lifestyle. Part of me was not willing to let go of bustling bookstores, busy coffee shops, and indoor produce markets where one could find any kind of cheese and fruit one desired. I liked being anonymous and enjoyed all the quirks of living in a city. I was used to the busyness, the rush, and the constant inflow of people. Noise was familiar, but silence was not.

Yet this was the life the Lord had given me, and I had accepted his offer. Surrender would come slowly in the form of daily prayer and walks in the luscious woods where an occasional fawn jumped into view. Instead of despising the quiet of the night, I stepped out to enjoy the stars I couldn't see in bright cities. Every time I wished to be somewhere else, I remembered the loneliness of noise and asked the Lord: "What do you want me to do?" Many times, I heard his voice in the brilliance of the full moon or the chatter of the crickets: "Be still, and know that I am God" (Ps 46:10).

• • •

Anna did not think her marriage would last only seven years and that she would end up in the Temple for the rest of her life. In her grief and suffering, the Lord called her to his service, and she accepted his offer of a life of chastity, prayer, and abstinence. Day after day, year after year, love for Yahweh guided her every step while she spread his love to those who visited the Temple. What the world would call stale and lifeless, the Lord blessed a thousandfold.

It is all too easy to fill out every minute of the day with an activity and fall prey to the god of busyness and productivity. We want to talk about how swamped we are with work, sports, school, or housework. We want to add one more thing to our to-do list, and soon enough everything that leads us to God is pushed aside, because we are afraid of the silence and the simplicity. We are afraid of being bored, or being in the company of our own thoughts, or hearing what the Lord might say about us, or being not enough. As we build that wall of fear and fortify it with chores and tasks, the Lord whispers, "My grace is sufficient for you, for my power is made perfect in weakness" (2 Cor 12:9).

Anna's example can lead us to a renewed appreciation of the Lord's presence, especially when life seems dull and things do not turn out according to our plans. In the footsteps of Anna, we can surrender to silence and simplicity, even as the storm of pain, godlessness, and confusion rages all around us.

If we are willing to stop the hurricanes in our hearts and minds to sit and pray in the temple of the Lord, the face of God will also be ours to behold.

Saint Anna the prophetess, pray for us.

QUESTIONS FOR REFLECTION

What distracts you most from recognizing where the Lord is showing up for you? List three things; then give them to Jesus in your prayer.

How can you remove some of the noise from your life?

Can you think of three simple ways to add more silence and prayer to your life?

3

Peter's Mother-in-Law

CAN YOU FACE YOUR SELFISHNESS?

Read Matthew 8:14–15

It didn't matter how much she tried to come back to the world. The commotion outside had grown so loud that even she, in the middle of her passing nightmares, could hear the begging and screaming of people. She wanted to get up and see what was happening. She wanted to chase away the crowd. She wanted a drink. Why was the water jug so far away? Why were her eyelids so very heavy? Why wouldn't the ceiling stop spinning?

She turned her head toward the clay jug and mug. Despite all her efforts, she could not even move her arm. Maybe a little more sleep would help. The crowd got louder. The ceiling became the floor. Her eyelids became lead, and the darkness claimed her once again. She welcomed the sensation of falling and letting go:

> And when Jesus entered Peter's house, he saw his mother-in-law lying sick with a fever; he touched her hand, and the fever left her, and she rose and served him. (Matthew 8:14–15)

She kept falling into the darkness without anything to hold on to or any bottom to reach. The further she fell, the more motionless she felt. Her old body was trapped in a dark, helpless world created by fire and sickness. Death would be welcome.

But death wouldn't come. Instead, in the depth of the night, a touch of light pierced her sick world. The impenetrable darkness was shattered, and in an instant, she was alive again. Where, a moment ago, she felt the touch of death, now life overwhelmed her. So much life! The fire that consumed her body disappeared like a feeble candle flame that was smothered under a gushing river.

She opened her eyes. The Lord's deep, warm eyes met hers. He gently held her hand as if she were something precious and fragile. A touch from his divine hands had taken away the sickness that had tortured her for days. The light of his power saved her from the darkness she kept falling into. In an instant, she was made new.

She sat up in the bed. Then standing up came as easily as breathing. The brand-new life in her made everything complete.

The Lord retreated back to his disciples. Her eyes followed him, and she wanted her whole being to respond to his gift. She wanted to stand up and serve the Lord, who was the source of all life.

The apostles, including her beloved son-in-law, watched in quiet reverence as their Lord defied death. Peter gave her a loving hug before he went back to the Lord and his friends. She took in the scenery, grateful for what she had been given. Then she reached out to the jug that just a short while ago had seemed so far away and gulped the cold water down before heading to the kitchen. She had to share the abundant life the Lord's gentle touch offered.

This is one of the first recorded healings of Christ. Whenever he touched a sick person, Christ demonstrated his desire to heal. But in the case of Peter's mother-in-law, what did she do when God-made-man touched her? Did she lie down again and seek to process it all from the comfort of her bed? Did she expect her daughter or others to tend to her? No. She got up and served Jesus and the disciples. She threw herself back into the lowly business of preparing food and cleaning up after dinner, even though, an hour before, she had been unable to stand up. This nameless woman received the healing touch of Christ and was transformed by it immediately, serving and loving selflessly like her Healer.

The nameless mother of Peter's wife presents us with a simple but wondrous path to follow. All those who are healed by the touch of Christ are called to a life of selfless service, not for the sake of their own glory, but for the love of God and neighbor. Yet most of us resent a nameless existence. We want recognition and appreciation. We have much to learn from Peter's mother-in-law. This woman's healing is recorded in all three Synoptic Gospels, yet her name is nowhere to be found. She remains known only by her relationship to Peter. This anonymity, however, is the reality of most of our lives. Our works go unmentioned. Our names go unknown.

• • •

I was not physically sick, like Peter's mother-in-law, but my soul and mind were crippled with the fever of a selfish and decadent life. Without the healing touch of Christ, I could not get out of myself to find the light. Without his gentle and persistent love, I could not even recognize the darkness within myself. By the time I became a mother, I had been healed by the power of Christ and the sacraments of the Church; the fever that imprisoned me was gone, but I was still standing by the bed, not quite knowing what to do. I may have taken a few reluctant steps, but most of them were, in the end, self-serving. The Lord had retreated and now waited for me to do what needed to be done.

When the overwhelming love and responsibility of motherhood hit me, the Lord beckoned me once again to join and imitate him, but selfishness tugged me back. Instead of rising and serving, I wanted to sit in the bed and nurse my wounds. I was healed. I was empowered to undertake this task of motherhood with the healing touch of Christ. But I didn't like being the unnamed mother of my kids. I wanted my name on books and academic articles. In his infinite divine wisdom, the Lord decided to show me my selfishness by using the beautiful gift of motherhood.

I read all the books. I watched all the instructional videos. I bought all the gadgets. I was ready to be a mom.

The first hiccup showed up when the ultrasound technician told me that the baby was breech. The all-knowing Internet directed me to put frozen peas on my belly, to lie upside down (it is as uncomfortable as it sounds), and even to try chiropractic treatments. I obliged. But, nope, the little man said no, and my first baby had to be delivered via C-section.

Morphine and recovery from such a major surgery were much harder than I expected, but I was grateful; many women undergo much worse experiences. Some even die during childbirth. My husband and I gave our son a Turkish name that means "rock," after Saint Peter, who has been continuously praying for this little man and his parents.

Being left alone at home with a tiny human being who was completely dependent on me and my husband was scary beyond comprehension. The responsibility weighed heavily on my shoulders every time he cried. The thought that it was up to us, his parents, to help him, soothe him, feed him, and keep him alive was at times paralyzing. It was just his daddy and I; there was nobody else.

Suddenly, all the books and videos seemed utterly inadequate. I was lost. Rock cried all the time. Breastfeeding hurt. I couldn't sleep. We couldn't watch this or that movie in the theaters. I couldn't take a shower in peace. The baby was everywhere, and he was everything. The cuddle time was wonderful, but when the night came and he was constantly fussy, we were helpless.

I never wanted children. Before Christ kicked some sense into me, I believed that this poverty-ridden, sexist world was such an awful place that bringing children into it would be one of the worst things one could do. Once, a boyfriend and I were riding the big city bus back home and he told me he would love to be the father of my children. We were both standing, our hands gripping those dangly things for balance. I could see his reflection in the window, the city lights twinkling in the distance. He was looking at me, but I could not look at him when I said, "I am never having children." He stared at me for a few more seconds and then returned his gaze to the darkness beyond the glass. We never talked about marriage and children again. My heart was stone.

Twelve years later, living with a newborn, I wanted to be back in the life in which everything went as I planned. I did not want to stay awake at night. I did not want to keep getting up to tend to the baby. I did not want to bathe him because it was too much work.

Don't get me wrong. I was a good mother, if you looked at me from the outside. I loved my son with all my heart. But there was a constant battle inside me. The dragon that had been fed throughout my self-centered life had grown so mighty that it was not yet willing to relinquish any power. Self is a strong thing. If not challenged, it will constantly feed off our sinful nature. This is exacerbated today, in our "me-before-you" culture. It is indeed a dragon that can be tamed only with grace, sacraments, and a life of service.

My life before Rock did not offer many opportunities for sacrifice. My husband is one of the most selfless men I have ever met, so serving him was not sacrificial. Actually, I loved cooking and cleaning for him, because I knew he would help me with the dishes and the laundry. It was reciprocal. With an infant, however, there is no reciprocity. I had never known such love.

Before this, I hadn't realized my dragon was even there. This pet that had been used to being fed nonstop became terribly apparent now that I had a vulnerable baby dependent on his parents for survival. I did not want to be selfless. I did not want to serve day and night. Rock could not even blow his nose, for goodness' sake. I needed to suction the snot out with a funny-looking bulb.

I had never cared for anyone without expecting anything in return. Every other love I experienced required reciprocity to stay aflame. Motherhood changed all that. Suddenly, I was not Derya: I was Rock's mother, and everyone in our little town came to know me that way.

At the height of those hard early days, my husband and I prayed the novena to the Holy Spirit. One single line in that novena slapped me in the face so hard that I, very badly, embroidered it on a cloth and framed it to be hung:

> He who is filled with the gift of Piety finds the practice of his religion, not a burdensome duty, but a delightful service. Where there is love, there is no labor.

"Where there is love, there is no labor." That is a constant reminder for me, even after five kids and ten years of parenting. Anything I do through love should be a blessing, even when it is unpleasant or accompanied by various bodily odors, because it is one more chance for me to serve the Lord: "Truly, I say to you, as you did it to one of the least of these my brethren, you did it to me" (Mt 25:40).

With every baby, I have moved one more step away from the bed, but more often than I would like to admit, the dragon of self roars. It wants to be fed again. It wants to be alone. It wants to yell at the children and complain about how hard life is. But then Peter's nameless mother-in-law comes to mind, and I picture her serving the King with utter gratitude. I remember to take a deep breath and read my inept embroidery once again: "Where there is love, there is no labor."

・・・

Where has your dragon made his lair in your life? If you were to put yourself in the place of Peter's mother-in-law, what keeps you tethered to the bed even after you've encountered Christ's healing love? What keeps you thinking about yourself? The world keeps telling us that we should "choose" ourselves above everything else and that we should scream our displeasure with everything and everyone, but Christ offers a different, more fulfilling life. Which lies of the world keep you from finding the fulfillment he offers?

Dear Peter's mother-in-law, if you are in heaven with your son-in-law, worshipping the Lord, pray for us to be willing, like you, to serve without holding anything back. And remind us to take a break from service now and then to meet a friend over chocolate and wine.

QUESTIONS FOR REFLECTION
What did you think of Peter's mother-in-law serving right after being healed? Would you do the same? Why or why not?

Can you think of specific areas where the Lord is beckoning you to leave your bed and serve?

Where do you think selfishness finds you most often?

4

Saint Photine

WHO DO YOU WANT TO BE?

Read John 4:1–42

The noon sun threatened to sear anyone who dared to wander in the open. Photine had no choice but to endure the trip to Jacob's well at the height of the day's heat. All the other village women came in the morning, while the cool of the night was still in the air. They gathered around with their pails and their rowdy children. Little boys ran around, chasing one another. Little girls clutched tiny, tattered dolls. Women talked about their husbands, about upcoming weddings, and about other women who were not welcome.

Samaria was too alien a country for the Jews of Judea, and too Jewish for the gentiles of Galilee. The Samaritan woman Photine was doubly alien in this world. She was one of those women whose life has been so marred by sin and misfortune that she had lost her place among reputable women. Her lot would forever be to draw water in the heat of the day, disgraced and alone.

Beads of sweat rolled down her back as she approached the small but generous well. Usually, she was the only one there at this time of day, but today, a man sat near the big, round rocks that led down to the life-saving water. Photine slowed her steps, because a woman of her reputation did not know what kind of conversation to expect from men. But she needed water, and she was willing to endure some unpleasantness for this task. Her back straightened with the expectation of rebuke.

Wait. The man was a Jew! She exhaled a sigh of relief — not because she expected better treatment from Jewish men, but because there was no way a righteous man of Judea would lower himself to talk to a disreputable Samaritan woman. She could handle disdainful looks to get her water.

Quietly, she approached the well, eager to leave as soon as possible. The man looked weary from travel and the heat. Beads of sweat rolled down his surprisingly kind face. The sun made the Samaritan and the Jew sweat without discrimination.

Photine lowered her pail into the dark depths of the well:

> There came a woman of Samaria to draw water. Jesus said to her, "Give me a drink." For his disciples had gone away into the city to buy food. (John 4:7–8)

Photine was startled. Was he talking to her? A woman? A Samaritan woman?

She squinted her eyes even more than the noon sun required,

staring at this stranger who was willing to deal with someone his people perceived as inferior. She wondered what was wrong with the man. Maybe he was delirious. Maybe he was one of those wanderers who lived a wild, detached life. Something was really strange about him, because a Jewish man would never ask a favor, even as small as a cup of water, from a Samaritan. Well, the disdain between the two peoples was mutual. She may have been disreputable, but she was still a Samaritan:

> The Samaritan woman said to him, "How is it that you, a Jew, ask a drink of me, a woman of Samaria?" For Jews have no dealings with Samaritans.
>
> Jesus answered her, "If you knew the gift of God, and who it is that is saying to you, 'Give me a drink,' you would have asked him, and he would have given you living water." (John 4:9–10)

What an odd thing to say. Photine tilted her head ever so slightly to examine this Jew who talked about living water. The man looked as if he had been traveling for a while, weary, yet strong. His shoulders slumped as if he carried the weight of the world. Other than that, he looked perfectly ordinary. Yet, instead of just leaving with her water, something made Photine question what he meant:

> The woman said to him, "Sir, you have nothing to draw with, and the well is deep; where do you get that living water? Are you greater than our father Jacob, who gave us the well, and drank from it himself, and his sons, and his cattle?"
>
> Jesus said to her, "Every one who drinks of this water will thirst again, but whoever drinks of the water that I shall give him will never thirst; the water that I shall

> give him will become in him a spring of water welling up to eternal life."
> The woman said to him, "Sir, give me this water, that I may not thirst, nor come here to draw." (John 4:11–15)

She chortled at this impossible offer of water that quenches thirst forever. The man was either a liar or a lunatic. What else could he be? She shook her head in disbelief at this madness, but something in his demeanor made her stay. His Jewishness didn't bother her as much anymore. Her hands mindlessly filled the water jugs, and crystal-clear liquid spilled over them. She wondered what kind of water would quench thirst forever:

> Jesus said to her, "Go, call your husband, and come here."
> The woman answered him, "I have no husband."
> Jesus said to her, "You are right in saying, 'I have no husband'; for you have had five husbands, and he whom you now have is not your husband; this you said truly." (John 4:16–18)

Photine's wet hands shook so much that the water jug slipped. The earth swallowed its contents in an instant, as she stared at the weary traveler with new eyes. How could this stranger see what was in her past and in her heart? Yet even though he seemed to know every ugly detail of her sinful life, he chose to commend her for the truth she had spoken instead of putting her down for her multitude of sins. He knew, yet he spoke to her. He knew, yet he was kind. This was no simple traveler after all.

The water jug lay on the muddy ground, forgotten. Photine dared to take a tiny step toward the man who claimed to be the Messiah. His face looked different somehow. Could he really be the anointed one? She did not let go completely at first, but his words had put a crack in the wall she had built around her. That tiny crack let a ray of light through, and her heart was filled with hope. Could a tainted woman like her encounter the Son of God in the middle of nowhere, while doing the most tedious of tasks?

When he told her who he was, she believed him — so much so that she left everything behind to tell people about the man who knew her ugly past but still offered forgiveness and hope. In that encounter at the well, Photine changed fundamentally. Before she picked up her water jug that day, she was a woman of shame and guilt who had to make the journey to the well under the noon sun. She had embraced the trap she had built herself, and since she saw no way out, she accepted her fate. A few minutes in the company of the Son of God, however, gave her a way out. She did not want to be the woman with many husbands anymore. She wanted to be the woman who told the people that she saw the face of God. What she was did not matter anymore; all that mattered was who she saw and what he gave her.

Photine became the first stone in the avalanche that eventually led many to recognize Christ and change their lives forever. According to tradition, Photine did not stop there. Her four sisters and two sons also converted and became tireless preachers of the Gospel. Under the persecutions of Emperor Nero, she was martyred. Christ emptied out this sinful Samaritan woman and replaced the darkness with so much light that she was willing to die for that weary Stranger.

• • •

Photine's story brings back a vivid childhood memory. During the Sacrifice Holiday of Muslims, my uncle and father used to slaughter a sheep for each family. At the end of gutting and skinning, my uncle would make a messy pile of sheep intestines on a rock. As the oldest children, my cousin and I were in charge of cleaning out and rolling up the squishy pile.

I would pick up the end, making sure to keep it as far away from my body as possible. With mouth firmly shut as if the yuckiness of the affair could somehow creep in, I would push the contents of the intestine forward by squeezing the slimy hose between my index and middle fingers. I am going to give you one guess about the contents. Yes, you're right. Tiny marble-size balls of sheep poop waited to be squeezed out every two inches or so. When I had a length of intestine long enough to roll, I would make loops like a garden hose.

After ten minutes of slimy agony, I would hand the neatly rolled sheep innards to my aunt. "Great, now we can make a ton of sausages!" she would say as she grabbed the still slimy but clean intestines.

Her sausages were to die for — fat links of spicy goodness made of flavorful lamb meat. They were the only reason I was able to put up with the unpleasant task.

This memory has come back to me often since I became Catholic. I don't really remember the smell or the slime anymore, but I do remember the taste of delicious sausage and fried eggs sizzling right next to them in the pan. Now, in the thick of life with many unexpected turns and twists, I remember the manure-filled intestine that turned into a casing for delectable sausages, because I am no longer the one pushing the tiny balls of poop out.

I am the intestine.

For a decade, I lived an utterly selfish life. After I lost all connections to Islam, and all the morality that the faith of my parents had enforced, there was no reason to control my appetites. I drank, smoked, used drugs, and had sex. The selfishness of a lonely life grew while pride in being somewhat smart and disenchanted fueled the flames of decadence. During that imperfect childhood and painful adolescence, my heart, mind, and soul were filled with lies and memories that needed to be discarded and replaced with truth and love.

As he did long ago for Photine, the weary Stranger at Jacob's well willingly and lovingly took on the task of pushing all that icky stuff out of me, so that I could receive the goodness he offered. Before my encounter with Christ, I was a woman who wanted to advance in life and become independent. My vision of a future life was limited, boring, and barren. When I met Christ at the well, however, he showed me that there was so much more to this life than being comfortable. There was eternity. He took the blinders off my eyes and has patiently been cleaning out my past so that I can have eyes for eternity. I did not want to be the woman who sinned anymore; I wanted to be the woman who shared the Good News, the woman who was open to life, the woman who loved recklessly, the woman who did not think about herself constantly. With his love and patience, with his words in the Scriptures, with his Church abounding in grace through the sacraments, Our Lord has been slowly — very slowly — turning me into a woman of grace.

...

Even though at times loneliness overwhelmed me during this journey — and sometimes it still does — I am hardly the first woman whose sinful past stood before her like a wall too tall to scale.

In a way, all of us are Photines. Whether we come from a wonderful Catholic family or have suffered through a dysfunctional and sinful past, at some point we all meet Christ at the well. And the Lord is always willing to deal with the hurts and scars of our past. As with the intestines I had to clean out for the sausages, he knows that the result is well worth the nasty work. With the insurmountable grace he offers, each one of us has the opportunity to claim his peace for our lives and move on to spread the truth about his love and mercy.

When you meet him at the well, what memories haunt you from your past? What prevents you from receiving his offer in full? If, for a moment, you were able to forget everything that took place before that encounter, who do you imagine or desire to be? If you are willing to take his offer, listen to his words, and be freed from sin, he will chip away what is holding you back from becoming like Photine.

I hope you've read the story of Eustace, the boy in C. S. Lewis's *Voyage of the Dawn Treader* who turned into a dragon because of his spiteful and greedy heart. No matter how much Eustace wanted or desired to, he could not become a boy again by himself. He had to let Aslan do it, he recounted, just as we have to:

> "Then the lion said — but I don't know if it spoke — 'You will have to let me undress you.' I was afraid of his claws, I can tell you, but I was pretty nearly desperate now. So I just lay flat down on my back to let him do it.
>
> "The very first tear he made was so deep that I thought it had gone right into my heart. And when he began pulling the skin off, it hurt worse than anything I've ever felt. The only thing that made me able to bear it was just the pleasure of feeling the stuff peel off. You know — if you've ever picked the scab off a sore place. It hurts like billy-oh but it is such fun to see it coming away.
>
> "'I know exactly what you mean,' said Edmund.
>
> "Well, he peeled the beastly stuff right off — just as I thought I'd done it myself the other three times, only they hadn't hurt — and there it was lying on the grass: only ever so much thicker, and darker, and more knobbly-looking than the others had been. And there was I

as smooth and soft as a peeled switch and smaller than I had been. Then he caught hold of me — I didn't like that much for I was very tender underneath now that I'd no skin on — and threw me into the water. It smarted like anything but only for a moment. After that it became perfectly delicious and as soon as I started swimming and splashing I found that all the pain had gone from my arm. And then I saw why. I'd turned into a boy again."

And it's not just about our pasts, because the Lord is more than willing and able to clean those out. This is just the first step on whatever journey we are on. Single or married, young or old, each one of us can accept the Eternal Water that quenches thirst forever.

Saint Photine, pray for us!

QUESTIONS FOR REFLECTION
If you put yourself in the place of Photine at the well and talk to Christ face to face, what keeps you from listening to him?

Who do you admire or aspire to be in life? Why?

How can you hear Jesus' voice better? What do you need to do so that you can be free to accept his offer?

5

The Bleeding Woman

DO YOU MEET GOD IN PRAYER?

Read Mark 5:25–34

Time is death.
Death is untouchable.
Blood brings death.
Blood is untouchable.
Every step she took required labor. Every task became insurmountable, every hill unscalable. She could feel the life-giving fluid leave her body once again. Her shame was constant,

but she didn't care, because the world kept spinning as the blood trickled down.

It had been years since she had been clean. It had been years since she had visited the Temple. It had been years since people greeted her with a genuine smile. She was unclean and untouchable.

Her brittle nails clung to the adobe bricks as she walked toward the crowd that was gathered around the man from Nazareth. The crippling exhaustion that dominated her days and nights would not stop her this time. With every step, dizziness threatened to overwhelm, but she didn't give in. The crowd looked like a roaring river between her and her salvation, for no physician and no amount of money had eased her burden. Instead, her hands grew colder and her face paler. She could feel the unwelcome breath of death on her neck.

She filled her tired lungs with fresh air and took another step into the crowd as she exhaled. She didn't need to talk to the Messiah. No. She didn't need to defile him with her uncleanliness. But if she could only touch his blessed clothes, her impossible sickness would leave forever.

One more step.

She could hear his gentle voice.

One more step.

She could see his dusty sandals.

One more step.

His robe swung back and forth as he walked and talked.

One more step.

She lunged in between the dusty legs of people she didn't know. Being trampled was not her worry. Missing this miracle was. She saw her own thin, yellow hand touch the hem of his garments. In an instant, as if the floodgates of a roaring river had been thrown open, life poured into her. The blood flow stopped. All was right. She stayed on all fours, listening to her body become right once again. Tears of joys flowed down her cheeks onto the dusty path:

> And immediately the hemorrhage ceased; and she felt in her body that she was healed of her disease. And Jesus, perceiving in himself that power had gone forth from him, immediately turned about in the crowd, and said, "Who touched my garments?" And his disciples said to him, "You see the crowd pressing around you, and yet you say, 'Who touched me?'" And he looked around to see who had done it. But the woman, knowing what had been done to her, came in fear and trembling and fell down before him, and told him the whole truth. And he said to her, "Daughter, your faith has made you well; go in peace, and be healed of your disease." (Mark 5:29–34)

The story of the Bleeding Woman is nestled in the story of the girl who died and was raised by Christ. Death and blood, two untouchables of Judaism. If you thought such concerns would stop the Son of God, you would be sorely mistaken. Of course, the poor woman did not know that Jesus would not care that she was an untouchable. He had come to heal the sick. She had been suffering from a bleeding disorder that rendered her constantly unclean. By extension, everything she touched was unclean. She did all she could to rid herself of this disease, but all was futile. We don't know for sure, but more than likely, she had lost her husband and whatever family she had. For twelve years, she was isolated from society, from her religion, and from her family. For twelve years, blood, the nectar of her life, drained out of her. One day, she heard about this Jesus, who healed the blind and cast out demons. She was sure that he would be able to heal her. All those years of trying to find a cure with no success did not drive her to despair.

Still, she did not dare approach him and his apostles openly. After all, she did not want to make them unclean or risk being rejected even before she could talk to the Teacher. But she was adamant. All she needed to do was to touch the hem of his clothes. His power was unlike anything she had ever heard of; surely a touch would heal her and make her clean again.

Consider her faith. Not only was she freed of her physical ailment, but the second Person of the Trinity commended her for her faith. I must confess that I would not have had her belief that one touch of his clothes would heal, especially when door after door had already been closed. Yet she would not give up. She simply refused to remain unclean. She reached out to Jesus.

Her simple touching of his garment was a prayer — a deep longing to be whole once again. She possessed an unfathomable faith that Jesus had the power to make her new.

• • •

Every one of us faces sickness, poverty, death, heartache, and hardship in this life. In this valley of tears, we don't always remember that the Healer is always within reach. All it takes is prayer, which connects our mortal hardships with our immortal Lord, who used his own crucifixion to save the world. Yet prayer is not easy.

It certainly isn't for me. I was lost and an inch from despair every time life did not go according to my plan. This was a constant struggle for me, as I had never learned how to make God part of my inner life. Those long decades of living as an atheist, relying only on myself and being skeptical of everyone around me had rendered my prayer life dry. I could read the theology books and learn the lives of the saints, but when left face to face with the Lord, I looked for a getaway plan. Reaching out to

Christ in time of need or in time of joy didn't occur to me. The Bleeding Woman portrayed such a contrast for me that I could not ignore her. My life, compared with hers, was perfectly heavenly, but the way I dealt with darkness and doubt was to turn in on myself and lock Christ out, even as he reached out to me with a healing hand.

I have learned three lessons from this woman who remains nameless in the Gospels.

First: *Don't lose hope.* We live in such a fallen world that sometimes the picture looks utterly bleak. Often, it is easy to see only the wrong and diminish the important things that are right. But there is a reason hope is one of the theological virtues. We know that the story does not end with the crucifixion, even though there may be a few days until the Resurrection. Daily, put your hope in Christ.

Second: *Reach out to the Lord.* Even when it feels as if he won't hear you, or it looks as if he is just passing by to attend to more important people, reach out to him. The omniscient Creator of the universe is waiting to hear from you, although he will not interfere with your free will. Jesus' heart is saddened when you go through this valley of tears by yourself. He wants to walk with you, but he will do so only if you invite him. Daily reach out to him in hope. A simple prayer will suffice.

Third: *Step up when he calls you.* The Bleeding Woman could have hidden when Jesus asked who had touched him, but she chose to expose herself to witness to others what the Lord had done for her. She had already been healed, and she could have disappeared into the crowd, but her courage bore witness to him. Like her, we are called daily to give thanks and share the hope that is in us.

• • •

Thanks to Adam and Eve's attempt to sever their ties with God, every passing moment brings all living things closer to death. This is not only a physical predicament, but a spiritual one as well. The only Person who can stop death once and for all is God, the source of all life, who conquered physical and spiritual death.

On this side of our own deaths, there is only one way we can keep our connection with the Lord: prayer. Prayer includes the sacraments of the Church, devotions, and personal prayers. Prayer establishes a constant communication line with the Lord, which draws us closer to Christ and leads us closer to eternal life.

To take advantage of this lifeline, though, we need to develop the habit of choosing to pray, despite our inclinations. This is how we nurture virtue in our lives. Daily prayer can feel long, tedious, and repetitive, but slowly that habit will bend our will toward what is good. (Still, I have a long list of excuses ready to be deployed when I want to binge-watch a show rather than pray.)

The *Catechism of the Catholic Church* describes virtue in a very succinct but effective manner: "A virtue is an habitual and firm disposition to do the good" (1803). The operative word here is "habitual." When I converted, I told my mentors, "I cannot wait until I am a Christian for ten years." I thought it was going to be much easier to follow Christ after I had a few years under my belt, as if one day suddenly a magical creature would bestow upon me the gift of virtue that would make saintly life a breeze. Little did I know that virtue is cultivated only by the constant repetition of good acts, which eventually form habits.

It starts with little things. For a long time, I found it very hard to get into a daily rhythm. Rolling out of bed with a grunt, then going downstairs to make coffee while kids played, only to stay in pajamas all day, was my habit of dealing with being a stay-at-home mother. Soon, an attitude of complaint seeped into every aspect of my life, until nothing I did gave me any joy. Then

I made one tiny simple change that completely altered this attitude. That one habit would shape the rest of my day. You may be expecting something revolutionary or deeply spiritual, but that one little habit was a daily morning shower. Yes, a simple shower right after I got out of bed changed my entire demeanor toward the day.

Then I pasted two prayers on the bathroom wall — a morning prayer and one my favorites, the *Stella Maris*. I started praying these prayers every morning after my shower, before I tackled the day. So, about twenty minutes after I rolled out of bed with sleep in my eyes and complaints on my lips, I was refreshed, dressed, and had my day oriented toward the Lord.

I wanted to keep reaching out to the Lord throughout the day, but often I forgot to or got lazy or busy. As Cardinal Sarah says in *God or Nothing*, however, we need to put the most important things in our lives first; otherwise, all the unimportant, trivial things will leave no room for God. Since spontaneous prayer did not come easily to me, I decided to make use of the endless treasury of Catholic prayers and devotions.

I started setting my phone alarm for noon to pray the Angelus, which is a very short prayer, and at 3:00 p.m. (the hour of mercy) to pray the Divine Mercy Chaplet. During the day, I made sure to pray at least one Rosary, either when taking a walk with the kids or when doing the dishes. I am nowhere close to praying all the mysteries in a day (though my husband does!), but perseverance has helped me take one baby step at a time toward becoming a more prayerful wife and mother.

Prayer, I have learned, is often like weight lifting. It is not easy for many, but if we want to train our prayer muscles, we have to go back to it, whether we want to or not. Building virtue takes time and perseverance, and, as G. K. Chesterton said: "If a thing is worth doing, it is worth doing badly."

Prayer is our lifeline to hope. We must renew it daily, or it will weaken and break in this world of sin. The prayer of Saint Teresa of Ávila is a powerful reminder for us to imitate the Bleeding Woman. Like her, we must daily reach out for the power of Christ and cling to the hope he offers:

> Let nothing disturb you,
> Let nothing frighten you,
> All things are passing away:
> God never changes.
> Patience obtains all things.
> Whoever has God lacks nothing;
> God alone suffices.

The Bleeding Woman here offers us the perfect model when we feel trapped and in despair, because she chose to neglect the crowd and the dirt to reach out to the Man who could heal her. When called out, she stood to talk to him face to face. If she could part the sea of legs to get to him, there was nothing to stop her from building the connection he asked of her. From then on, his divine face would be the only one she turned to in times of joy or suffering.

QUESTIONS FOR REFLECTION

Do you relate to the Bleeding Woman? If so, how? Have you ever waited a long time for healing, only to find it in Christ?

What stops you from meeting God in prayer?

Can you list three things that hinder your prayer life, and can you offer solutions?

6

Justa

WHERE DID GOD FIND YOU?

Read Matthew 15:21–28

In this book, I will call her Justa, as she is known in the Orthodox tradition. The Gospel account of the Canaanite woman's encounter with Christ is uncomfortable, unless we read it with a proper understanding of who Jesus is.

We hear about Justa in the Gospels of Matthew and Mark. Jesus sought some time away from the crowds in gentile territory, but those who heard of him would not leave him alone:

> And Jesus went away from there and withdrew to the

> district of Tyre and Sidon. And behold, a Canaanite woman from that region came out and cried, "Have mercy on me, O Lord, Son of David; my daughter is severely possessed by a demon." But he did not answer her a word. And his disciples came and begged him, saying, "Send her away, for she is crying after us." (Matthew 15:21–23)

Justa was at her wits' end over the evil spirit that tormented her daughter. What was a mother to do? She heard of this man who cast demons out and healed people. There was one problem, however: He was a Jew, and she was a gentile, a Greek. When the news spread that this Jesus of Nazareth had come to her land, where Jews were not usually received well, all she could think of was how she could persuade him to help her daughter. The accounts of his miracles were unbelievable, yet she believed them.

It was not a secret that Jesus did not want to see anyone, but she could not wait any longer, for this might be her only chance to see the miracle worker. Justa had the humility to look for God even when he was a stranger to her people. Any sacrifice would be worth it, if her daughter would be saved. At the sight of the unassuming man whose deeds had crossed tribal boundaries, she threw herself at his feet. It mattered not that his people did not like her people or that she was a complete stranger. Here was the solution to her problems; but she still had much to learn:

> He answered, "I was sent only to the lost sheep of the house of Israel." But she came and knelt before him, saying, "Lord, help me." And he answered, "It is not fair to take the children's bread and throw it to the dogs." (Matthew 15:24–26)

Wait! What? Did he just call her a dog? In the third millennium, we want to straighten our backs and wave our index fingers at the Word of God. Who does he think he is? But Justa knew who he was. The mere act of falling to her knees before this man showed her humility. Still, Christ, whose Incarnation was the ultimate act of humility, wanted to show her that she needed to go even further. Instead of taking offense and letting her pride get the better of her, Justa recognized the one to whom she spoke and realized that everything he would say about her would be true. She was — as we all are — nothing but a dog at the master's table. Christ taught her true humility and so led her to wisdom.

At the same time, Justa teaches us:

> She said, "Yes, Lord, yet even the dogs eat the crumbs that fall from their masters' table." (Matthew 15:27)

The conversation was not about her daughter anymore; it was about who she was in comparison with the Son of God. Justa may have thought she had risked much by seeking him out, but her humility was not nearly complete. Christ, who was more than willing to answer her prayer, wanted her to learn this lesson in self-awareness and wisdom by embracing her status — a status all of us share as mere human beings — as a dog at the Lord's table. Jesus, who would soon embrace the humility and torture of death on the cross, would answer her prayer:

> Then Jesus answered her, "O woman, great is your faith! Be it done for you as you desire." And her daughter was healed instantly. (Matthew 15:28)

Justa placed herself under the table like a dog. For her humility, Christ raised her, a gentile and a woman, to the level of the children of God.

Some suggest that this gentile woman taught Jesus a lesson

in mercy and the universal nature of his salvific mission. This suggestion is, of course, outrageous, as Christ's human will was in complete harmony with his divine will. We humans — sinners — have nothing to teach the Second Person of the Trinity. We must strip away the discomfort caused by our twenty-first-century sensibilities in order to read this Gospel passage. The question we must ask is not what Justa taught Jesus, but what Jesus was trying to accomplish in his encounter with her.

It seems in this story that it was Justa who was doing the searching and pursuing. She needed a healer and was willing to make whatever sacrifice was necessary for her daughter. In her mind, all Christ had to do was to sit at the table and wait for her arrival. Yet she was not the one who did the finding in the end. In her heart, Justa didn't know that it was God who had gone to great lengths to reach her. When she realized the kind of humility the Lord desired, she arrived fully at his doorstep, not just for her daughter, but for herself as well. It was the Son of God who sought and found this lost sheep, not the other way around.

• • •

The British Airways employee told me that my one big suitcase, in which I had packed my entire life the night before, was too heavy. I did not have the money to pay for the extra weight, so two of my favorite sweaters ended up in a trash can in the airport, and the other two went over the three layers I was already wearing. Good thing I like being toasty.

In an unexpected turn of events, a little over a month prior to this departure, I received a scholarship from a prominent university in England. Before I knew it, the short few weeks had flown by, and the time had come to take the airplane to an unknown city with unknown people.

Looking back, I wonder whether I was getting too comfortable in Ankara, where I had been living for almost a decade. I was accepted for a Ph.D. program in the same prestigious university where I received my M.A. Most of my friends would stay in the same university as well. My dormitory, the library, even the restaurants would stay the same. The church, at whose doors I had tentatively knocked to finally talk to a Catholic priest, had become a regular destination, even though it took an hour and a half to get there. Living in that bubble was what I wanted, but was not what God had in mind when I was granted that scholarship and made the decision to move across the continent.

Part of me dreaded leaving the comfort of the familiar, but getting a doctorate in England would help me to get a much better job in Turkey. As a Christian, there was no way the Turkish government would trust me, so I could not hope to occupy high positions like those of most of my non-Christian friends. To be successful, I needed a degree from a respectable institution. Also, the scholarship came out of nowhere, because I had not applied for it. The department was low on female students, so the administration decided to offer incentives to them.

I also looked forward to living in a country where Christianity was not so out of the norm. Living in Turkey, I did not understand what was happening to faith and morals in the West. The Christians I knew in Turkey, Protestant and Catholic, were outstanding followers of Christ. Despite their personal faults, there was no doubt Christ was at the center of their lives. In my naiveté, I assumed Christians like them would be the norm in the West. Surely, even if Hollywood and the media were not friendly to Christianity, everyone else still clung to Jesus. I longed to be part of a cultural majority and to see churches around every corner.

With these dreads and hopes, I left behind my cherished life in Turkey and took the few-hour plane ride to a different world. Until the day I moved, I had never traveled to England, a land of fairy tales and times long past, but the scenery was everything I imagined and more. From the window of the train from London to Durham, the scenery turned from alluring to breathtaking — from rolling green hills, to towns, and then Durham Cathedral came into view. I had never seen a building so full of majesty and intricacy. Nestled in the luscious northeastern greenery, one of the finest examples of Norman architecture reached to the sky. During my first few weeks, I took many walks among tall trees covered in vines and moss, and along the deep, slow river. Durham was the most magical place I had ever been — so much so that even Oxford and London failed to impress. When I got too tired from long treks, I would find a tiny tea shop or a pub to stop in and just look around. It was as if someone had transferred me into a fairy tale where scones and crumpets, ales and ciders, and tea were plentiful.

The first time I visited Durham Cathedral was not disappointing either. Even though this seat has not belonged to Catholics for centuries, its history is a testimony to missionary spirit. In the land of saints such as Cuthbert, Aiden, and Venerable Bede, in the cathedral that was built at their behest, I took in the high arches, the intricate masonry, and the smell of stone pillars and old books. Visitors spoke in hushed voices, because even those who did not believe could see the beauty and the reverence that true devotion can inspire. Many hours I spent there, reading, praying, and thinking, and it never became mundane. This cathedral, built a thousand years ago, was still able to fill my third-millennium heart with awe.

After the first month of newness and novelty passed, however, and tea and crumpets became part of the daily routine, I began to realize that the Christianity I thought I would find in the West had left long ago. There is a scene in *The Lord of the Rings* where King Elrond tries to explain to his immortal daughter the folly of marrying a mortal man. In case you are not familiar with the story, Arwen, the elvish princess, is in love with a mortal,

Aragorn. Her father tries to persuade her to leave with the rest of the elves before darkness begins to reign in Middle Earth:

> Whether by the sword or the slow decay of time, Aragorn will die. And there will be no comfort for you, no comfort to ease the pain of his passing. He will come to death an image of the splendor of the kings of Men in glory undimmed before the breaking of the world. But you, my daughter, you will linger on in darkness and in doubt as nightfall in winter that comes without a star. Here you will dwell bound to your grief under the fading trees until all the world is changed and the long years of your life are utterly spent.

In the movie, as Elrond speaks to his daughter, the scene flashes to an old but beautiful Arwen wandering around in a forest like a ghost. She is still alive, but forgotten, because all who knew her have passed away. That scene, I realized after a while, was the perfect depiction of Christianity in England. There were unmistakable signs of a glorious past everywhere: stunning cathedrals, beautiful churches, crosses in signs, street and pub names starting with "Saint," but everything was a shadow cast behind something long since gone. That realization did not take away the beauty and the enjoyment, but it opened my eyes to the reality of being a Christian in the twenty-first century in the West. No matter where I went, Christ would remain an outcast, and so would his true followers.

I knew Jesus and what he had done, but I needed to go to a foreign land, live among foreign people, feel lost, and then, in that loss, look for him once again. As I reflect on it, I believe my journey was similar to the Canaanite woman's road to Christ. My humiliation came in the form of loneliness. I expected to find a vibrant Christianity that would fulfill my desire to belong and be part of the herd, but instead I found ghosts and specters, and utter loneliness that made the long nights even longer. Like Justa, I had gone in search of a cure for my ailment, but there was only one person who could satisfy my heart.

Thankfully, my problem was not as severe as Justa's, but I had hoped to get rid of all the insecurities and the constant reminders that Christians did not belong in Turkey. In Ankara, every time I took a walk around the campus that overlooked the city, I pictured a spiritual cloud suffocating everyone within. Christians lived in the shadows and talked in whispers. My friend who led me to the Catholic Church crossed only his heart when he ate in public, because a full blessing would turn too many heads and cause too much trouble. Turkey, my home, was a land where I had to hide the most important thing in my life. In my innocent imagination, I had pictured England as a place teeming with Christians. I thought I was going to find God, but all I found was silence. With silence came the burden of loneliness.

I soon realized that I was more alone in the home of Saint Cuthbert than in the conquered lands of Asia Minor. In that brand-new life in a foreign country, not only had I lost the friends who had become my family, but my disillusionment with the state of Christianity in Europe reached its completion. I was a dog under the table, watching the children of God slowly leave the table while crumbs became more and more scarce. Justa sat next to me, patting my back, probably with a smile, because her encounter with Christ would repeatedly remind me that being a little Christ requires humility and persistence. My Lord had to remind me who I was without him so that I could be complete with him.

...

Many of us think we are chasing after Christ. We pour ourselves into our families. We volunteer at our churches. We make sure that Christmas looks picture perfect and the kids' outfits coordinate for Easter. We suffer for family and friends. But it is always the Lord who pursues us, even when we have walked many miles to find him. Justa's encounter with Christ invites us all to remember that he wants a deeper connection with us, a connection that can come only through humility.

When the suffering and challenges of life take our breath away and we run to him who can deliver us, sometimes the answer we hear is not what we want. Yet, just like Justa, we should remain at Christ's feet and trust that when all the ages have passed, his wisdom will remain. We can also remember the psalm: "Be still, and know that I am God" (Ps 46:10).

QUESTIONS FOR REFLECTION

Do you feel as if you have been chasing after Jesus in your life? Is it possible that he is really the one chasing after you?

What challenge or suffering in your life might help you get closer to him? Have you experienced sufferings in the past that brought you to his feet like Justa?

How might Christ be challenging you to embrace humility in your life as a Christian? What holds you back?

7

Saint Mary Magdalene

WHAT LIES DO YOU BELIEVE?

Read Luke 8:1–3; John 19:25; 20:11–16

The voices of the darkness kept talking to her, day and night. When she was awake, she had no peace. When she was asleep, she got no rest. Her mind was a tiny room, occupied by many others besides herself. The others never slept, never rested, and never stopped torturing her. She was lost, despised, and abandoned. Lies and despair pressed in from all sides. Loneliness was her fate forever; loneliness in the middle of so many voices.

She took a bite of the freshly baked bread that a kind woman had given her. She could feel the inviting warmth of the loaf in her hands, but the soft pieces turned to ashes in her mouth. Every sip of water was dry. Hers was an endless desert.

She thought there was no one to save her until the Son of God one day visited her city:

> Soon afterward he went on through cities and villages, preaching and bringing the good news of the kingdom of God. And the Twelve were with him, and also some women who had been healed of evil spirits and infirmities: Mary, called Magdalene, from whom seven demons had gone out. (Luke 8:1–3)

I cannot even begin to comprehend what it means to be tortured by seven demons — the darkness, the hopelessness, the despair Mary Magdalene lived in every single day. Each minute must have felt like an eternity. She must have been an outcast, defiled and unwanted. More than likely, her conscience was silenced in the presence of evil spirits and habitual sin.

One day, a man, a simply dressed Jew with a large following, spoke to the demons inside her with such authority and power that the spirits left her for good. The prison walls that entrapped her for as long she could remember crumbled at the sound of Christ's command. His divine voice did not simply make a crack; no, he turned the brick walls into dust and night into day. How blinding and exhilarating it must have been to be finally free! The voices that tormented her day and night were forever silenced.

Imagine the first night of silence and the restful sleep.

Most of us are tormented with lies. Some of these lies have been told to us by other people; often, they are the lies we tell ourselves. The deception becomes such a big part of us that we build walls for self-preservation, only to trap the demons inside with us. No matter how far we run, no matter how loud we shout, the whisper of sin binds us to a life without light — that is, until the

Light himself frees us, just as he freed Mary Magdalene.

• • •

As a little girl raised in a Muslim household, I often found comfort in reading the Quran and reciting the prayers. When I could observe the monthlong fast during Ramadan, I was filled with pride. Rising before dawn to eat so we could endure the daylong lack of food and drink was something special. I savored the tahini bread and sweet red tea. A child's heart wants to walk toward God, no matter how misguided a religion is. The exploits of Muhammad or the unapproachableness of Allah were not things I bothered myself with. All I wanted was to please my master with an innocent joy and a bendable will.

When that innocence was ripped away and sin became a real, regular, and wounding part of my life, I felt even more trapped in the small town of my childhood. By American standards, this town was big, but it remained rural in many ways. I thought that if I lived in a bigger and more civilized city, I would be happier. After all, surely movie theaters, universities, libraries, and trendy coffee shops would fill the gaping hole in my heart that got bigger with every passing day.

By the time I was eighteen, I was a self-professed atheist and communist, and traditional morality had left my conscience. All I had was a vague sense of injustice that made me angry at the bourgeoisie and people with money. Everything unattainable was to be torn down. I looked at people who had more than I did, and I was mad with envy. I had no understanding of sin, and my Islamic upbringing had not provided me with a proper understanding of fallen human nature. As the years passed, the heart of that innocent girl who was oblivious to what sin could do became hollowed out. It was up to me to fill the emptiness with something — anything, really. My own sinful nature obliged, no doubt with many a whisper from the father of lies. The demons of my own making started to settle into my empty heart as my head filled with the lies about who man is and who God is.

One of the first lies that pitched a tent with secure spikes in my mind was about my womanhood. In Eastern cultures, it is more desirable that the firstborn child in a family be a boy. I was a first child, but alas, not a boy. Then came the lies of Islam that say women are inferior and should be subject to men. One of my Quran teachers, a woman, told me that a fiery sword would torture me forever for every strand of hair that escaped my hijab. But I wore a hijab only during Quran lessons. That meant an eternity of millions of fiery swords, or however many hairs were on my head. Unfortunately, I have very thick, wavy hair. Did exposition of wavy hair require scimitars, rather than long swords? I was not sure.

When I lost my faith in Islam, these lies about my womanhood did not disappear; instead, they took a different shape. Without a proper understanding of being created in the image of God, I thought power-hungry men invented the supposed difference between men and women to suppress women into submission. Difference meant inequality in my mind. To be truly equal, man and woman had to be the same, and any variation was simply an imposition of the society.

As it happened, this demon had many tentacles. On the one hand, I saw men as enemies of women, not to be trusted or followed. On the other hand, I felt an insatiable longing to receive men's approval. Talk about a love-hate relationship.

The urban environment suited my desire to live in the shadows, on the outside of society. I believed that God — if there was a God — was oppressive, uncaring, and carnal, making the masses bow before him without reason or love. My solution was to hide, instead of searching for the truth. What better place to hide than in a herd, like sheep? Among millions, who would ever know about the darkness that brewed inside me? Who would care what

I did with my life or whether I enjoyed drinking until everything felt numb?

The demon that whispered in my ear unceasingly about my worth, my womanhood, and my inferiority became a very good friend of the demon who said that God would not love me even if he existed. I kept feeding those demons with more lies and more rebellion. The crowded city was the perfect habitat for me and the deceptions that flourished in my young heart.

Six months and many heartbreaking disappointments later, I realized that the demons I fed had packed every lie they knew into brand-new luggage and moved in with me. Where I went, there I was with my lies, demons, and misery. The tentacles reached even beyond the soul-cleansing waters of baptism and unifying oils of confirmation. For years, I didn't trust the godly men the Lord put in my path, even though marriage was my desire. I wanted to be a wife, but I was not willing to relinquish my selfishness in the service of a man. Being single meant I could not be hurt, but the desire for intimacy grew stronger. The tentacles pushed me so strongly in different directions that shadows shrouded even my brand-new marriage. While a part of me wondered whether my husband would leave at the slightest sign of discontent, another part of me wanted to show him that I (and only I) was the center of my life.

This struggle was not dominant enough to paralyze my daily life, but it was strong enough to keep me from surrendering either to being a single woman or to being a wife. Discontent lingered for a long time until I saw what Christ was trying to do in my life. I would not learn for a long time that for me to be truly happy, I needed someone stronger than I to tell me the truth about myself and cast those traveling demons out. I was very much like Mary Magdalene.

When Christ's light entered my life for the first time, a sense of relief and freedom followed. That quiet and subtle peace after many years of turmoil was so welcome that for days, sleep was more restful, food more delectable, and water more sweet. The truth of God and his Son had freed me from the lies, but this freedom would be an ongoing work.

Mary Magdalene was my example of how to keep the demons out while growing in holiness. I looked to her as she stood with Jesus during his brutal Passion:

> Standing by the cross of Jesus were his mother, and his mother's sister, Mary the wife of Clopas, and Mary Magdalene. (John 19:25)

The woman whose life was changed drastically by the touch of Christ would not leave the side of the God-man even as he underwent execution. Even after everyone, including Peter, left, Mary Magdalene stayed with Our Lady and Saint John, watching Jesus give up his life so that many might be freed from the oppression of sin.

How could she leave? She knew what awaited her if she did not follow Jesus. She knew that even though her demons did not have a hold on her anymore, the only way to avoid temptation was to stay at the foot of the cross. For her faithfulness, despite her sinful and demonic past, the Risen Lord would appear to her on Easter. On the day of his resurrection, Mary Magdalene found the tomb empty. At once, she informed the disciples, who, after having seen the empty tomb and the folded burial clothes, went home:

> But Mary stood weeping outside the tomb, and as she wept she stooped to look into the tomb; and she saw two angels in white, sitting where the body of Jesus had lain, one at the head and one at the feet. They said to her, "Woman, why are you weeping?" She said to them, "Be-

> cause they have taken away my Lord, and I do not know where they have laid him." Saying this, she turned round and saw Jesus standing, but she did not know that it was Jesus. Jesus said to her, "Woman, why are you weeping? Whom do you seek?" Supposing him to be the gardener, she said to him, "Sir, if you have carried him away, tell me where you have laid him, and I will take him away." Jesus said to her, "Mary." She turned and said to him in Hebrew, "Rabboni!" (which means Teacher). (John 20:11–16)

Mary dared not leave, even when Christ was tortured, crucified, dead, and buried. The tomb was empty, and all she could think about was that she must retrieve his body. She probably did not understand why Jesus did not save himself as he had saved so many others, but she remembered the demons, the sinful life, and the darkness. She owed Christ such a debt that her gratitude would not — could not — let her leave Jesus even after his death.

Mary's demons whispered lies about who she was and where she belonged. They confused her so much that she didn't know who she was at times. When the Lord cast out her demons, her soul and mind were clean and clear for the first time she could remember. She clung to Christ during his earthly life and was present on the day of his glorious resurrection. The only way to stop believing the lies and hearing the whispers was to be near her Savior, and he remained close.

∙ ∙ ∙

That is the kind of faithfulness and love every daughter of God should yearn for, because he has broken the chains of slavery to sin. Now that we are free, we can freely follow him and stay at the foot of the cross.

Each of us believes in lies that keep us in the dark. "You are not good enough. You are not worthy. You don't pray enough. You are not holy enough. You are not a good wife, mother, or sister. You are not pretty enough. No one will ever love you." But the closer we get to Christ, the more trivial these concerns become. We start seeing ourselves in the light of his love. While we realize that we are not worthy of the gifts Christ has given us, we also become more aware of how unconditional and unlimited his love is.

Thankfully, we are never alone in this journey to the heart of Christ. The Mother of Our Lord is always there to guide us under the protection of her mantle. Like Mary Magdalene, we should always ask for the hand and intercession of the Mother of God, who brings souls to her son.

Yet this is also a lifelong process. Mary Magdalene shows us how true this is; not only did she stay with her Lord, but she also remained close to his mother. According to the Greek Church, Mary Magdalene moved to Ephesus with Our Lady and Saint John to live out the rest of her days. For her, being close to Jesus meant being close to Mary, and the formerly demon-possessed sinner knew all too well the cost of being led astray.

When the demons of my past whisper in my ear that I am a worthless sinner, that a life of motherhood is nothing but a social construct, that freedom is an illusion, I run to the foot of the cross to stand with Mary Magdalene, a former sinner like myself, for Christ has made all things new.

Saint Mary Magdalene, pray for us.

QUESTIONS FOR REFLECTION

What lies do you hear in your head about who you are?

What truth that comes from Christ do you have hard time believing?

Where can you meet Mama Mary on this journey?

8

Saint Martha

CAN YOU HANDLE THE MUNDANE?

Read Luke 10:38-42; John 11:17-27; 12:1-3

Everything had to be perfect. The Lord had graced her house with his holy feet. She ran to the kitchen in haste to make sure that there was enough food and drink for the Lord and his disciples. She dished out hearty soup into wooden bowls and searched for the wooden spoons that went with the beautiful bowls. Mary had used them last. Where did she put them?

For that matter, where was Mary, anyway? She couldn't

believe that her sister left her alone to tend to such important guests by herself. She could use help, but help was nowhere to be found. She found the spoons in a pot, newly washed. Carefully, she placed each bowl on the tray, making sure to arrange it just right. It looked perfect. She'd serve some refreshing cold plum juice later. The sweet drink would be perfect for a warm day like this. She would have to find the ornate jug her brother bought for them. Only the best for the Lord.

She pushed the creaky door with her shoulder while she carried the tray full of soup bowls. Her eyes fell on Mary immediately, and anger rose in her throat. Mary was sitting on the floor, listening to the Lord, as if the duty of serving him rested only on Martha's shoulders. She took a deep breath, but bitterness would not leave. Surely, the Lord would have a thing or two to say about such laziness and selfishness:

> Now as they went on their way, he entered a village; and a woman named Martha received him into her house. And she had a sister called Mary, who sat at the Lord's feet and listened to his teaching. But Martha was distracted with much serving; and she went to him and said, "Lord, do you not care that my sister has left me to serve alone? Tell her then to help me." (Luke 10:38–40)

Martha's frustration with Mary might seem unreasonable or unfair to Western ears, but hospitality has always been paramount in the Middle East. In Turkey, from an early age, all children, especially girls, are trained in the ways of hospitality. As soon as someone steps into our house, we are all expected to stand and wait until the guest is seated. We are not allowed to put our feet up or cross our legs in the presence of a guest. One must always have something to offer to the guest, at least a cup of water or a glass of tea. One of the most challenging tasks of my early childhood was to master the skill of carrying a cup of water without touching the sides so that a guest could grab the beverage easily.

Needless to say, it would be unthinkable for a Middle Eastern woman to sit at the feet of a guest, especially an esteemed guest like Jesus, instead of running around like a headless chicken to make sure that he was attended to properly. Martha wanted to tell Jesus, "I am serving you while she sits and does nothing":

> But the Lord answered her, "Martha, Martha, you are anxious and troubled about many things; one thing is needful. Mary has chosen the good portion, which shall not be taken away from her." (Luke 10:41–42)

The Lord is eternally patient with us. Jesus does not tell Martha that what she is doing is not important or that the physical needs of a family or guests can be ignored; instead, he tells her to leave her worries and anxieties at his feet. If Martha had asked Mary for help, the Lord may not have interfered, and Martha would have gotten the help she needed. Instead, Martha tried to make Jesus approve of her frustration over Mary's quiet attitude of listening. Our Lord did not tell Martha to stop serving, because he was not talking about the chores, but about Martha's attitude toward the work and her sister. He told her to leave her worries with him, instead of brewing a strong pot of resentment.

Being a carpenter's son, Our Lord was aware of the necessities of life and the tedium of the daily grind. Consider how long it takes to carve things out of solid wood with nothing but axes and chisels. In the family home, he watched his immaculate mother cook, clean, sew, and do it all over again. The tedium and the desire to escape the mundane is part of the fallen world. Jesus meant to teach dear Martha not that her work was evil, but that the way we approach our work can either glorify the Lord or harden our hearts toward those we serve. That's why Jesus encouraged Martha to do one thing over all other things: to be always present at the feet of Christ.

This is true for all of us, regardless of our vocation in life.

Saint Martha must have understood what Jesus told her that day, because when we hear about her again at the time of Lazarus's death, her faith is rock solid:

> Now when Jesus came, he found that Lazarus had already been in the tomb four days. Bethany was near Jerusalem, about two miles off, and many of the Jews had come to Martha and Mary to console them concerning their brother. When Martha heard that Jesus was coming, she went and met him, while Mary sat in the house. Martha said to Jesus, "Lord, if you had been here, my brother would not have died. And even now I know that whatever you ask from God, God will give you." Jesus said to her, "Your brother will rise again." Martha said to him, "I know that he will rise again in the resurrection at the last day." Jesus said to her, "I am the resurrection and the life; he who believes in me, though he die, yet shall he live, and whoever lives and believes in me shall never die. Do you believe this?" She said to him, "Yes, Lord; I believe that you are the Christ, the Son of God, he who is coming into the world." (John 11:17–27)

By the time Lazarus died, Martha had heard and witnessed many extraordinary things about Jesus and his ministry. Unlike countless others, however, she took the Lord's words to heart, and rushed to him when her beloved brother died. Her words to Christ are a witness to her faith, but she, not Mary, was the one who ran to the Lord. She was always the one in action, whether serving or leaving the house of mourning to meet the only One who has power over death.

Martha's personality had not changed, nor had the daily requirements of her life, but this time she ran to the Lord not with a complaining and discontented heart but with faith and hope. That remarkable change in her attitude opened her eyes to who Jesus is. "Yes, Lord; I believe that you are the Christ, the Son of God" were her words as she mourned the death of a brother. She did not complain and demand with rolling eyes, but instead approached her Savior with confidence and reverence. Now that she had reclaimed the joy of her salvation, the Lord rewarded her with one of the most powerful phrases found in the Gospels: "I am the resurrection and the life; he who believes in me, though he die, yet shall he live, and whoever lives and believes in me shall never die" (Jn 11:25–26).

•••

The reality of the fallen world and our fallen nature often leads us to behave like Martha toward her sister. For me, the whining started when I settled into the life of a mother with constant laundry and dishes. It was amazing that children needed to be fed at least three times a day. Who knew! In between meals, there was always a toy to be stepped on or the result of some bodily function to be cleaned up. The cycle ended with bedtime, only to begin all over again before birds started chirping.

To be honest, my little ones did not offer much intellectual stimulation, either. Building LEGO towers and singing "The Wheels on the Bus" endlessly meant that each day looked like a gray, dreary carbon copy of the day before. Before long, the humdrum became so unbearable that I lost all sight of the blessings of my life.

For a long time, I did not understand why the mundaneness

of life bothered me so much. After all, everyone's life consists of some tedium. My complaint was not that my life was hard, because, let's face it, Lego towers are not that challenging (unless you get into building dinosaurs). I was weary of the stability that was the basis of the tedium. I struggled with an unsettled heart and mind without being able to identify the problem.

I bought a book as a gift for the priest who had baptized one of our babies. After the book arrived, it sat in my car for a while before I could deliver it to the good father. One day, as I waited for my son to come out of his school, I picked up this book. It talked about a sin I had never properly understood before. Little did I know that the restlessness in my heart was the ever-growing sin of acedia. How could I fight it, if I did not know what it was?

Dom Jean-Charles Nault's excellent work *The Noonday Devil: Acedia, the Unnamed Evil of Our Times* summarizes this far-reaching sin of our day: "On the one hand, acedia is a sin against the joy that springs from charity; it is sadness about what ought to gladden us most: participation in the very life of God. On the other hand, acedia is a sin against charity when it crushes or paralyzes activity, because then it effects the deepest motive force of activity, namely, charity, the participation of the Holy Spirit."[*]

The results of rampant acedia not only influence our daily lives as children of God, but that lack of joy infects everyone around us and eventually cripples our ability to carry out Our Lord's last instructions to his Church — namely, to share the Gospel, starting with the domestic church. Father Nault talks about the desert monks and how their hearts were not content within the confinement of their cells, and they would want to leave the desert and encounter new worlds and new lives. The monks called these temptations to abandon their calling the "noonday

---

[*]Dom Jean-Charles Nault, *The Noonday Devil: Acedia, the Unnamed Evil of Our Times* (San Francisco: Ignatius Press, 2015), 80.

devil," because this demon's oppression peaked around noon, when fasting and penitence became unbearable.

I dare say my life — the life of a mother who has a washing machine and a dishwasher and does not have to leave the house to use the bathroom — cannot possibly be compared to the life of a desert monk, but the temptation to flee is the same. Just like the monk, I was called by God to a specific vocation, and I accepted that calling. The Lord poured grace upon grace on me to share the joy of my salvation, starting with my husband and children, and hopefully beyond.

Father Nault suggests a few remedies we can all use to counter the creep of acedia in our lives: stability, remembering, and joy.

Stability. Our first instinct when acedia creeps into our hearts is to desire change. It is no wonder that we hear phrases like "she fell out of love" or "we needed a change" or "we in a rut." Instead of keeping the promises we have made, we let our current — and very changeable — whims dictate our lives. Then we find ourselves in need of more change. Instead of giving in to that urge to seek constant change — even to the point of leaving our mundane lives behind — we must stop and, in silence and reverence, remember the immutable Lord, who is forever faithful. We must ask for his stability. When our hearts want to run away, we must hide ourselves in his faithfulness and love, found in the Mother Church. When I feel overwhelmed with a desire for a change, I make every effort to pray in front of the Blessed Sacrament, and Christ *always* calms the storm in my heart and helps me see more clearly. Instead of giving in to the urge to run away, emotionally or physically, the Eucharist helps me plant my feet firmly in Christ and his Church while the tornado passes over and the skies become clear again.

Remembering. Remembering is the antidote to our forgetful nature. In the Old Testament, the Lord often tells the

Israelites: "Do not forget!" If there is one thing the sons of Jacob have in common, it is that they forget over and over how faithful the Lord has been and how many times he has saved them from slavery and from themselves. Of course, the same forgetfulness remains in us. To help us remember, Father Nault prescribes an increased adherence to the Eucharist: "The Eucharist is what gives temporality its ultimate meaning, since it takes up the past, the present, and the future: love never passes away." The Eucharist reminds us not only of the Lord's faithfulness, but of our own promises to live out our vocation. These promises were made after thought and prayer, and we must hold on to that determination rather than give in to fleeting forgetfulness.

Joy. The final remedy for acedia that Father Nault suggests is joyful perseverance. The psalmist, who undoubtedly suffered from acedia at times, prayed, "Restore to me the joy of your salvation, / and uphold me with a willing spirit" (Ps 51:12). This short line has become a frequent prayer on the lips of this twenty-first-century mother who often forgets God's faithfulness. One of my all-time favorite pictures about God and what heaven might be like for us comes from Chesterton's *Orthodoxy*:

> Because children have abounding vitality, because they are in spirit fierce and free, therefore they want things repeated and unchanged. They always say, "Do it again"; and the grown-up person does it again until he is nearly dead. For grown-up people are not strong enough to exult in monotony. But perhaps God is strong enough to exult in monotony. It is possible that God says every morning, "Do it again" to the sun; and every evening, "Do it again" to the moon. It may not be automatic necessity that makes all daisies alike; it may be that God

makes every daisy separately, but has never got tired of making them. It may be that He has the eternal appetite of infancy; for we have sinned and grown old, and our Father is younger than we.

Saint Martha's example teaches us what acedia looks like, so we can fight this most stealthy of sins with her example. When the worries and the tedium of our daily lives overwhelm us so much that all we can muster are words of complaint and images of darkness, we must remember to say a prayer to Saint Martha and try to shake ourselves out of the oppressive rot of acedia. Then we can commit (or recommit) to following the three steps described by Father Nault and keep pressing forward with fidelity to our call.

• • •

On this side of death, we will always be surrounded by the mundanity of life and its shallow dissatisfaction, but until we experience the innocent joy of children in heaven, we need to learn to orient our hearts to joy and do "little things with great love." This often requires a conscious change in our attitude as we work to get our emotions in line with our wills and as we get used to serving with love and gratitude.

In heaven, we will not be bored by repetition, nor will there be any tedium. We will not suffer from the acedia that is caused by our sinful hearts. In heaven, the hole in our hearts that causes us to be dissatisfied will be completely filled. We shall be forever young. We shall be forever joyful. We shall forever enjoy every sunrise.

For each one of us to get there, Saint Martha, pray for us!

QUESTIONS FOR REFLECTION

When you read the story of Martha and Mary, how do you react to the sisters? Do you tend to sympathize more with Martha or with Mary? Why?

Do you struggle with acedia? How does this spiritual struggle affect you in your daily life?

Name one or two mundane tasks in your life that you struggle to perform with joy. What are some concrete steps you can take to change your attitude?

9

Saint Joanna

CAN YOU SERVE WITHOUT RECOGNITION?

Read Luke 8:1–3; 23:55; 24:10

A giggling group of young women entered the kitchen, clad in silky fabric, talking about the evening's feast. The baker's brows wrinkled as she stirred the cake batter. Something must have gone wrong. Joanna thought about inquiring but decided not to. It was better to let her concentrate. A young boy carried in a basket of bright-pink turnips, stealing a glance at the girls. Joanna tasted a pastry stuffed with crushed walnuts and dates. The baker stopped for a moment to see her reaction. Her pink cheeks broke into a smile at the sight of Joanna's approval.

Herod's house was a big one to run and manage, but Joanna's husband undertook this task with precision and the utmost attention. Joanna was the wife of Chuza, who oversaw the affairs of the house of Herod Antipas, the Roman-imposed ruler of Galilee. In all likelihood, Joanna came from an upper-class family and had lived a life of privilege. When she married Chuza, she moved to Galilee, which is not far from Nazareth, Christ's hometown.

This woman, who was the wife of one of the most powerful men in the area, living in comfort and luxury, heard about Jesus of Nazareth. He healed the sick, gave sight to the blind, and raised the dead. In the hustle and bustle of the busy household of a ruler, she must have witnessed the shallowness of a life of wealth and decadence. This Jesus, who could do things only someone with unbelievable authority could do, provided something much more fulfilling than the life in Herod's home, where drunkenness, adultery, and indulgence ran rampant. Not only did she have to live in the midst of Herod's sin-ridden household, but Scripture indicates that she was also afflicted with either evil spirits or some incurable sickness:

> Soon afterward he went on through cities and villages, preaching and bringing the good news of the kingdom of God. And the Twelve were with him, and also some women who had been healed of evil spirits and infirmities: Mary, called Magdalene, from whom seven demons had gone out, and Joanna, the wife of Chuza, Herod's steward, and Susanna, and many others, who provided for them out of their means. (Luke 8:1–3)

We don't know what her infirmity was, but we know that Jesus healed her. On one of her darker and sicker days, maybe Joanna thought that this Jesus, about whom she had heard countless stories, would be the one who would save her from the incessant affliction.

And he did.

She was free from her pain, both physically and spiritually, because this man healed people inside and out. How oppressive it must have felt to go back to the darkness of Herod's home, despite the delicacies and the finest silk! That was the day she became a follower of Christ.

Saint Luke names these women to note that Jesus' ministry had many invisible hands supporting him as he humbled the proud and chastised the self-righteous. The Son of God did not worry about whose toes he stepped on. As he spoke the truth and invited everyone into the kingdom of God, behind the curtain, influential women such as Joanna and Susanna supported him financially, maybe even pulling a few strings here and there to make sure he had what he needed.

Joanna encountered the healing power of Christ firsthand. Because of that divine meeting, her life changed, and how could she ever forget that? She couldn't. That is why, even after the apostles scattered, she and other women gathered what was needed to tend to Christ's broken body that Sunday morning:

> But on the first day of the week, at early dawn, they went to the tomb, taking the spices which they had prepared. And they found the stone rolled away from the tomb, but when they went in they did not find the body. While they were perplexed about this, behold, two men stood by them in dazzling apparel; and as they were frightened and bowed their faces to the ground, the men said to them, "Why do you seek the living among

the dead? He is not here, but has risen. Remember how he told you, while he was still in Galilee, that the Son of man must be delivered into the hands of sinful men, and be crucified, and on the third day rise." And they remembered his words, and returning from the tomb they told all this to the Eleven and to all the rest. Now it was Mary Magdalene and Joanna and Mary the mother of James and the other women with them who told this to the apostles; but these words seemed to them an idle tale, and they did not believe them. (Luke 24:1–11)

Christ had changed the lives of these women so drastically that even after his death, they would not leave him. Because of that loyalty, Joanna is called "the Myrrhbearer," and because of her unwavering faith, she was one of the blessed ones who discovered the empty tomb and heard the messenger of God speak about Jesus' resurrection. The Holy Myrrhbearers are the women who were involved in the burial of Our Lord and found the empty tomb. But Joanna did not seek this honor. She did not ask to become one of the few women who are named in the Gospels. Her life was changed forever, and she left at the feet of Christ the glory that this world could offer. Her healing, her works, and her devotion were all shrouded in silence. Her embrace of an unremarkable life of serving Christ behind the curtain is an inspiration for all of us not to be afraid of a hidden life.

• • •

Sadly, as I battled my concerns about what others would say if I chose to stay at home for my family, I did not appreciate the simplicity of silent service like Joanna's.

"The gate of heaven is very low; only the humble can enter it," Saint Elizabeth Ann Seton said, but humility is not an easy lesson to learn. Pride resists it like the child who is about to get a vaccine. When the Lord nudges me toward humility, all I think about is the hurt, not the good. The Lord prepares this lesson in different ways for each of us, but the outline is the same: Let the Son of God be your compass by dying to yourself over and over again. For me, one of these deaths came in the shape of letting go of a professional career as an academic.

Neither Islam nor atheism gave me an accurate view of who I was according to God. I learned to rely only on myself. I studied, received degrees, and worked toward the goal of financial independence, which I believed was the best way to stand up to the men in power. I had no proper understanding of man, woman, the Fall, sin, and grace. In Islam, women were considered inferior and defective. Muhammad himself said that hell will be filled with women. My life in Turkey had attested to the fact that men will dominate women when their religion justifies the oppression and exploitation of women. To me, all religions were the same, because I was never taught otherwise.

As an atheist, I confused equality of men and women with sameness. At the same time, I blamed men for all the problems in the world. My worldview was so askew that I thought the only way to find freedom was through financial independence. I held this view even though no boyfriend of mine — thankfully — had ever tried to oppress me.

My rather confused and distorted mindset ran deep, so deep that even after I became Christian, most of these ideas about myself lingered under the surface. I had a lesson to learn, and humility would be my true teacher.

The Lord sent me a husband who had a job that could support his family. A few years into our marriage, I finally received my doctorate, and as a husband and wife with two children, we were faced with the decision about what I should do with that degree. We had already decided that one of us would stay at home with the kids. My husband was willing to stay at home, if I was able to find a job equal to his so that we would have financial security and good insurance.

Enter ego and the Lord's lesson in humility.

My mother, who lives thousands of miles away, called me almost every day to ask whether I had a job yet. She was worried that my American husband would one day leave me, and I would be stuck penniless with the children. The experience of her past haunted our relationship. More importantly, however, she wanted to brag about her daughter. Despite her failures as a parent, she still wanted to live through us, especially through me, as she had bragged about my education for years, only to see me become a stay-at-home mom. She was humiliated, and I felt small.

That was only the beginning. The next humiliation came when I realized that my salary and benefits would never match my husband's salary as a state employee of fifteen years. We wanted a big family, and we wanted one parent to stay at home. Children eat a lot and poop into diapers that must be bought with hard-earned cash. Even in the most generous of situations, my income as an entry-level professor would never be as high (nor the benefits as good) as what my husband could provide.

The final humiliation broke the back of the camel that was me. There was a job opening at a good Christian university not far from where we live. I thought it was the perfect job for the family and for me. Over the years, I had learned not to pray for material things, since frequent moves and lack of disposable income had made me relatively detached. But this time it was different. This time, I prayed and prayed and prayed to get this job. I spent hours in front of the Blessed Sacrament, begging the Lord to give me this job. But a curious thing happened; the more I prayed to get this job, the more restless my heart became. In the presence of the same Christ who promised us that his yoke is light, the storm in my soul became visible even to me.

Months passed, and I did not even get an interview request, let alone the job. But with every week I spent pounding at this door that was not meant for me, the vision of a toddler having a temper tantrum for a fifth cookie came to mind. "Thy will be done" had become a prayer to be said only in the Our Father during the Rosary and at Mass; I did not want to pray it for such an important decision in my life. That was it. My life and my desires — essentially my will — trumped everything else, including the Lord's will for me and for my family.

This epiphany was striking. I took a deep breath as I stared at the golden doors of the tabernacle with the engraving of a chalice and a host, light pouring out of both, and I slowly exhaled. The prayer came out of my mouth sincerely for the first time in months: "Thy will be done."

Then I was free. The boulder I had been trying to push up the hill disappeared, and the mountain was not that steep anymore.

That surrender was only the beginning of a long journey in which humiliation led to freedom, but where would this freedom that said, "I will go wherever you take me" end up? I did not know, and despite the lightness, I was apprehensive. Could I actually leave the self-satisfaction of being a professor and telling people what I did for a living? After all, changing diapers and building LEGO towers did not sound as impressive as teaching at a university. Could I be content with living a simple and unrecognized life, where nobody called me "Doctor" and all the clothes I owned had stains from various bodily fluids?

It is with sadness that I remember those days of not being willing to let go of my pride, when I listened to the loud noise of the world instead of the gentle whisper of the Lord. In the moments of utter humiliation, the Lord cut open the wound that kept festering and telling me that success and money would make me happy. Once surrender and acceptance brought freedom, then the joys of motherhood started to reveal themselves.

Of course, parenting day and night was not easy, even with the support of an amazing man. It was particularly difficult to tell people (especially my mother) that I had made the choice to stay at home with the children. I stopped looking for work and settled into my new life, which was, in fact, not new at all. I had already missed enjoying the first year of my daughter's life by focusing on the wrong thing.

No, motherhood was not easy, but it was good.

Being present and available has been one of the best gifts I could give to my little children. But my kids were not the only beneficiaries of this surrender. My marriage — not I — once again took the center stage, and I became a more pleasant and peaceful person as I let go of the grumpiness of not getting what I wanted. The raging storm calmed down, and the Lord used the tool of humiliation to teach me the lesson that his will is better.

Sometimes, being "just" a mother is still uncomfortable, even though it does not matter that the world measures my worth differently than the Lord does. But signal graces of little kisses and mispronounced words through the day remind me often why God gently led me to a life of rebellion in a materialistic culture. This rebellion of mine is not worthy of newspaper articles — a life of simplicity rarely is. I cannot even take credit for finding this peace and calm after such a storm, because I did not want it; I was simply given an amazing gift. Motherhood in the midst of laundry piles and chewed-up books turned out to be an oasis in the desert of a success-driven life.

Had I paid more attention to the women in the New Testament, I would have seen what the Lord valued above all else. Had I followed Joanna's example closely, I might have realized

I could be content serving Christ without being seen and recognized. Had I understood what a responsibility it is to be in charge of eternal souls, I would have fallen to my knees in worship for the privilege.

・・・

As it happens, I am writing this chapter on Monday of Holy Week, when we all start to contemplate how to become less like our sinner selves and more like the divine Son. By attaching ourselves to Christ, we have taken the first step toward that holiness, but there is more — much more. We are called to be different, otherworldly. Archbishop Charles Chaput of Philadelphia wrote this reflection on Holy Week in 2018: "This week is Holy Week, and the original Hebrew meaning of that word 'holy' is *other than*. God's ways are not human ways. They are *other than* ours; higher and better, more powerful, moving and redemptive than our own."

Joanna is a role model for the modern woman, who is expected to be glamorous and important. Having been healed inside and out by the Son of God, she can teach us that true freedom and love can be accomplished only in the shadow of Christ, who will humiliate us into peace and calm. We cannot reach our true goal in the limelight of a decadent culture. Joanna knew that the road Christ invites us to walk is indeed steep, but at the same time, it is infinitely better than anything we can concoct for ourselves and for the world. We are called to be other, and if we will answer this call, then, like Joanna, who went to tend to the lifeless body of Jesus, we, too, will witness the Resurrection of the Son of God.

Saint Joanna, pray for us.

QUESTIONS FOR REFLECTION

What in the little that we know of Joanna's life inspires you the most?

Why do you think the Church emphasizes the need to serve without recognition? Do you know of any other saints who witnessed to this with their lives?

Where in your life do you crave recognition most? Why? How can you lay that desire at the feet of Jesus?

10

Saint Priscilla

ARE YOU WILLING TO BE A CO-MISSIONARY?

Read Acts 18:2, 18, 26; Romans 16:3;
1 Corinthians 16:19; 2 Timothy 4:19

White cobblestones disappeared under her feet as she rushed to the house where her husband and many others waited for her return. The market was louder and busier than usual, but what was most important was the news that Emperor Claudius was getting impatient with all the disturbances in the city. The floggings and imprisonments were rampant already;

what more would they do? Priscilla did not dare to imagine. All she wanted was to get home, to the relative safety of the crowded, blessed house she shared with her husband.

The wooden door creaked on its hinges when she pushed it closed behind her. A sigh of relief escaped her mouth, and her shoulders relaxed. She was home.

Aquila must have heard the creaky old door, because he ran to his wife for an embrace. His arms closed tightly around her, and all was well for the moment. This was the man who was always at her side, loving, caring, and protecting. Life's worries seemed smaller when he was around. Yet, when he finally let her go, there was concern in his dark, warm eyes. Priscilla took a deep breath and closed her eyes as he relayed the bad news.

The emperor had finally had enough. No Jews were allowed to stay in Rome. Priscilla and Aquila would have to leave behind their home, their friends, their trade, and everything they had established, at the word of an agitated man who did not care at all about them. The task overwhelmed her for a moment, but then she saw only confidence and surrender in her husband's eyes. His faith comforted her. Once again, she was grateful for the companion the Lord had given her:

> After this [Paul] left Athens and went to Corinth. And he found a Jew named Aquila, a native of Pontus, lately come from Italy with his wife Priscilla, because Claudius had commanded all the Jews to leave Rome. And he went to see them; and because he was of the same trade he stayed with them, and they worked, for by trade they were tentmakers. (Acts 18:1–3)

Not long after Christ's death and resurrection, there were recorded problems between Jews and new Christians. Emperor Claudius did not care what the problems were, nor was he interested in the differences between Jews and Christians. As far as he was concerned, the problems were caused by the Jews, so he threw the baby out with the bath water and expelled all the Jews (including Christians) from the city of Rome. Aquila was one of those innocents who had to uproot his whole life and put down new roots in a new land across the sea. He traveled to Corinth with his wife, Priscilla, whose name always appears right next to her husband's in Scripture. Corinth was where the Apostle Paul met and stayed with this couple.

Were they already Christians when Saint Paul came to stay with them, or did they convert because of that encounter? We do not know, but we know that husband and wife shared the same profession as Paul: they were tentmakers. Aquila probably learned how to make tents during childhood as an apprentice, since every Jewish boy was supposed to learn a trade from a young age. Tentmaking was no easy trade then — not like sewing together the nice waterproof fabrics of the twenty-first century. Goat hair, which is very resilient but hard to work with, was the main material used.

Most of us do not have the luxury and the blessing to work in the same profession as our spouses, but we can imagine how loving, caring, and selfless Priscilla and Aquila's marriage must have been, if they spent day and night together, all the time. They were each other's best friends, especially when an unknown future awaited them in the aftermath of their exile by Claudius. They had each other, and they had a trade; their physical location was a secondary concern.

They ended up in Corinth, where they met Saint Paul, who had traveled to Corinth from Athens during one of his missionary journeys. Since Paul continued to make tents to support his mission, he more than likely met fellow tentmakers wherever he went.

Scripture tells us that Priscilla and Aquila's journey did not end in Corinth. They had the privilege to travel with Paul:

> After this Paul stayed many days longer, and then took leave of the brethren and sailed for Syria, and with him Priscilla and Aquila. At Cenchreae he cut his hair, for he had a vow. And they came to Ephesus, and he left them there; but he himself went into the synagogue and argued with the Jews. (Acts 18:18–19)

What Priscilla and Aquila had was a common mission as husband and wife, which created the intense and beautiful scenes in the recent movie *Paul: The Apostle*. They accepted the task the Lord gave them and proceeded forward even when darkness and doubt crept in. In the movie, you can also see how Paul and Luke were co-missionaries in the field. This was a dangerous profession that often claimed the lives of Christians. Each one was tasked with spreading the Gospel to the gentiles, even when the shadow of death loomed over them in a hostile city.

The Lord can ask us to be co-missionaries with a friend, a sibling, or a work partner, but in Priscilla's case, it was her husband. They shared not only the same trade but also the hardships of being exiled and living in an environment where Christians were not welcome. Her life would look not like the life of a comfortable woman, but like the life of a missionary, a life filled with strife and with much grace. Priscilla and Aquila wandered from city to city, guiding and leading the people of God as a godly couple.

•••

When I got on the airplane that took me from Ankara to London, I expected to be back in Turkey in four years, looking for a job as a professor. There were two things that I was very certain of then: my faith and my plans to come back and be a missionary in my own country. In a matter of two years, all that would change when Virg and I drove a red truck from Texas to our current town, where we would live after the wedding.

I felt as if I had let everyone down: Turkey, the Turkish church, all the people who expected me to come back, and even Christ.

At the same time, however, I was sure that Virg was the man I wanted to marry. All through our correspondence and talks, we prayed and asked for the intercession of Our Lady, Saint Joseph, Saint Bernadette, and Saint Irene. We both felt that our union would be a blessing for both of us. Even after all that prayer and the assurance that I was in love with this wonderfully Catholic and selfless man, the thought that the Lord needed me in Turkey, not in America, kept bugging me. At the time, I did not see it as pride. Looking back, I see that the idea that the Creator of the cosmos would need my help is laughable. But back then, laughter was the last thing on my mind.

Part of this guilt was no doubt self-inflicted, since, despite being a relatively new Catholic, I was already on the way to perfecting Catholic guilt. I thought that by leaving Turkey, I was being selfish and even running away from a fight. I put marrying this guy before serving my country, and wasn't that self-centered? I also saw myself as a coward because I had chosen an easier life. Another part of this guilt came from others, though: my friends had encouraged me to come back and were disappointed in my choice of an American husband.

All this guilt kept stewing under the surface, simmering away, while Virg and I went through marriage preparation. Looking back, I realize that these hidden feelings were clear indicators that I had not yet embraced my new role as a wife. To become a wife meant that I had to yoke myself with an actual person and this person's mission. It did not help that I was almost thirty and a little too independent for my own good. The result was that guilt had a mighty fertile soil in which to take root and grow.

Marriage is hard work. Sin and selfishness wait at every turn to break our resolve to unite ourselves with another. Of course, the father of lies hates this union that God has chosen to create souls and forge a strong society. Thankfully, the Lord had shown me the importance of yoking myself with someone who put God above all. My husband and I were equally yoked, but even then, shedding my former self to surrender completely to this unbreakable union was very hard. This is true for many marriages. We do not want to let go of what we were in order to become what the Lord wants us to be through the vocation of marriage.

The concept of marriage remained in a nice box in my head with many Scriptures and even a good understanding of *Humanae Vitae*. I mean, what else did I need to know in order to get married? My approach to marriage was not unlike reading the manual of a car and then thinking that I was ready to drive. (My two failed driving tests at the age of thirty-one will bear witness against me in any court of law.) What I did not yet realize was that the mission of *my* life seemed more important to me than the mission my marriage demanded. It was a confusing transition. I needed the example of saints such as Priscilla and Aquila, who served the Lord together.

Both Virg and I came from broken families and converted as adults. Before we even agreed to talk on Skype, we made sure that we were on the same page about the most crucial aspects of our lives. We talked about contraception, tithing, and even abstaining from meat on Fridays. At the same time, unlike Priscilla and Aquila, we had very different backgrounds regarding education and profession.

After Priscilla and Aquila's conversion, the Lord continued to use whatever talent they had to enhance his kingdom. There was no way for me to learn my husband's trade (he's a law enforcement officer — no, thank you), and I'm sure the same is true for most of us in our marriages today. But most of us can imitate Priscilla's willingness to become a co-missionary with her husband, even in challenging and unsettling situations.

Once their close friend Paul spread the Good News in Corinth, the new believers started to gather in Priscilla and Aquila's house. "The churches of Asia send greetings. Aquila and Priscilla, together with the church in their house, send you hearty greetings in the Lord" (1 Cor 16:19). The couple's exile from Rome could not have been easy. Everything they worked for and accumulated had to be left behind because of a few troublemakers. Instead of constantly looking back and thinking about what might have been, however, the tentmakers jumped with both feet into their new life. Not only would Saint Paul benefit from their friendship and hospitality, but the entire church of Corinth felt the warmth and generosity of this faithful couple. Their marriage, perfected through their faith in Christ, would become a blessing to people all around them, regardless of their earthly location.

These co-missionaries knew that our Creator does not worry about time and space. We run into problems in carrying out our missions when we forget this. That was exactly my problem. Not only did I think the Lord needed me to convert the Turks, but I also thought I would be useless to his kingdom if I failed. My illusion was so complete and distorted that, at first, I did not want to get my American citizenship, thinking that such an act would seal my betrayal.

Once the wedding in Turkey was over and we recovered from the swine flu (which we contracted in a swine-free Muslim country), I slowly started to settle into my new life. The man whom God had given me as a partner and friend for life was one of the godliest and most prayerful people I had ever met. As my false and arrogant anger toward myself lost its control on me, I realized that Virg was trying to teach me his trade: a simple life of prayer, through which we would become missionaries together. Married life became our Corinth, the unexplored territory. If I was willing to open my heart, the Lord would use my generosity and hospitality to reach others, even though I felt untethered.

Still, a part of me wanted to stay behind and look back instead of embracing the adventure with the partner the Lord graciously gave me. This reluctance to surrender myself completely created pressure in my relationship with Virg — nothing major, but little things that could roll into an avalanche if not dealt with properly. The problem with me was that, because I held back, subconsciously I looked for ways to be right all the time, or reasons to be offended. I always went for the negative conclusion, instead of the more likely and charitable one.

During the first few months of our marriage, I started to pray the Rosary daily, because it was an indispensable part of my husband's prayer life. His devotion to Our Lady inspired me, as a woman and as a prospective mother, to learn more about the Mother of God. My husband's patient guidance and countless prayers slowly helped me to let go of the plow in order to firmly join hands with him. After many regrets and apologies, I learned four things that first year of marriage, and these are lessons that I think can apply to any of us in this vocation to become co-missionaries:

> **Give each other the benefit of the doubt.** This means "don't be easily offended." Try to let the emotions calm down, then ask yourself whether he actually meant what you perceived.

> **Let the little things pass by.** Living with someone else is hard. Don't make mountains out of molehills. Ask yourself: "Will this matter a year from now?" "How im-

portant is this in the grand scheme of things?" Let your selfishness stand aside.

Hold your tongue. If you are very angry or agitated, say a Hail Mary; don't speak in anger.

Pray with and for your co-missionary.

As I surrendered to his plan, God surprised me with my new mission territory. It did not take me long to see Christianity's slow retreat from the United States. It started to sink in that even this land of freedom was a mission field, and my husband and I were called to be co-missionaries wherever we were. All we needed was to offer our humble talents and short lives to God so that he could use us to further his kingdom.

• • •

Regardless of where you are in life (married, single, engaged, religious), the Lord does not want you to labor alone. If you are married, hopefully to a faithful Catholic man, your co-missionary lives alongside you to fulfill God's plan for you and your family. If you are single, a friend or a co-worker or a sibling or a parent could be your co-missionary to serve the People of God. Sometimes, we feel lonely in this walk, but there is always another soul we can build friendship with and find comfort in. It may be easier to turn in on ourselves and become prey to self-pity, but if we are willing, the Lord will provide a co-missionary for all of us. When the struggles of life and our mission burden us, Priscilla and Aquila's example can guide us to become united in work, prayer, and love with our co-missionaries. Priscilla shows so clearly the importance of truly becoming one with our spouses and walking with the Lord hand in hand, in whatever mission field he chooses for us.

When we are trapped within ourselves and opt for that lonely journey instead of traveling with others, let us remember the words of Blessed Carlo Acutis: "Sadness is the gaze turned towards oneself, happiness is the gaze turned towards God. Conversion is nothing but moving the gaze from the bottom to the top. A simple movement of the eyes is enough." Let us remember to move our eyes toward the Lord, who is always willing to provide us with comfort and help. How can we see his wonderful providence if all we do is gaze at ourselves?

Saint Priscilla, pray for us, along with your husband, Saint Aquila.

QUESTIONS FOR REFLECTION

Think of a time when the Lord asked you to trust him through very hard times. What happened? Who were the co-missionaries he placed in your life to help you through?

Do you have a co-missionary in your life now? If so, how can you improve your relationship with that person? If not, what can you do to find someone to share the journey?

Are there times when you find your gaze focused on yourself? How might Jesus be gently inviting you to look to him instead?

11

Saint Lydia of Thyatira

WHAT WILL YOU DO WITH HIS GIFT?

Read Acts 16:11-15

The shellfish that released the intense purple had been boiling for a while now. Everything in and around Lydia's house smelled of its unpleasant but welcome odor. Collecting hundreds of shellfish and then boiling them in giant vats until they released the bright and lucrative shades of purple and red was an arduous task, but the outcome fed Lydia and her entire household. The Lord had blessed her, and she was grateful to the one God she had learned about some time ago — likely from the Jews of her acquaintance. She did not know much about this God, but she knew he was above all the gods of her land. She wanted to know more.

The odor of shellfish still hung in the air as she and a few others walked down to the river, where the Jews gathered on the Sabbath, for theirs was a town without a synagogue. Lydia liked being near the water and the trees, where the air was fresh and she could hear about the Creator of the universe in the serenity of his creation. She found a sturdy rock at a distance where she could still hear what was being spoken. Today, the speaker was a man named Paul:

> Setting sail therefore from Troas, we made a direct voyage to Samothrace, and the following day to Neapolis, and from there to Philippi, which is the leading city of the district of Macedonia, and a Roman colony. We remained in this city some days; and on the sabbath day we went outside the gate to the riverside, where we supposed there was a place of prayer; and we sat down and spoke to the women who had come together. (Acts 16:11–13)

This man Paul was different. Lydia had not seen him before, and the words he spoke were nothing like anything she had heard before. You could cut the silence with a knife when he talked about what he had done to stop a group of people called Christians from talking about a man named Jesus, the Christ. His eyes filled with tears when he talked about hearing the voice of the One whom he had persecuted. The more he talked, the more people hung on his every word. Could Paul really be speaking to them about God's anointed one?

One often heard about different men claiming to be the Messiah, but this Jesus whom Paul spoke about was different.

Paul's words came with knowledge, wisdom, and authority. The men who were with him witnessed the truth of what he said. Lydia's hands wrapped around her red dress, and her knuckles turned white with anxiety and excitement, for she knew in the depths of her heart that Paul had brought them the Word of God. This Jesus of Nazareth was truly the Messiah. As the river rushed by them and the birds sang their pleasant songs, Lydia knew that the God she had worshipped all these years had just changed her life:

> One who heard us was a woman named Lydia, from the city of Thyatira, a seller of purple goods, who was a worshiper of God. The Lord opened her heart to give heed to what was said by Paul. (Acts 16:14)

Lydia did not move until people cleared away slowly, some nodding, some in deep thought, and some shaking their heads as they walked away. Her eyes did not leave Paul and his friends, because this was the moment she had been yearning for all her life. This was the moment God had chosen to redeem her and her household. It was a gift. An unexpected and overwhelming gift, but a divine gift nonetheless. She whispered a few quiet words to one of the servants who had joined her. The lad walked away and then returned with her entire household. The servants muttered in whispers as they rushed to their mistress's side. Lydia had made up her mind.

She stood up with determination and walked to Paul. She held the hands that once persecuted the Christians but now traveled the world to spread the Good News. Today would be the day when Lydia would become part of the fold and join the Christians — the little Christs:

> And when she was baptized, with her household, she be-

sought us, saying, "If you have judged me to be faithful to the Lord, come to my house and stay." And she prevailed upon us. (Acts 16:15)

Lydia of Thyatira was one of those women whom God found in an unlikely place, even though she had been seeking him her whole life. There is no mention in Scripture of a husband, father, or brother, which means Lydia was probably widowed. She may even have been divorced, which was not uncommon back then, yet she was financially comfortable. The purple goods she sold were used mostly by the wealthy and the elite, because purple dye was hard to obtain. The fact that she was a seller of purple textile and she owned a house big enough to host Paul's party along with all her household hints at her material prosperity.

We learn that she was a worshipper of God, meaning that she was a gentile. So, here we have a wealthy woman who rejected whatever belief system she grew up with in order to follow the one true God revealed to the Jews. She was not lost in the worldly things she could afford or the elite society she could keep. Instead, on the Sabbath, humbly, she walked out of the city gates with the Jewish women to pray and seek the face of her Creator.

The Lord honored her desire to be a woman of God by sending her Paul, who probably did not expect to preach to women that morning. He simply followed where the Holy Spirit led. Lydia had heard, likely even read, about the history of God's people. When this Jewish man came down to the river with his followers and talked about the Messiah, who died and rose from the dead for the Jew and the gentile alike, Lydia found her true home. Her search had ended; the Lord had sent her a teacher who guided her closer to God.

•••

When I imagine Lydia listening to the sounds of nature along with Paul's voice, I remember the day the Lord gave me my own gift. At that time, I could not decide whether to follow Christ or not. I was standing at this crossroads with my mind hazy because of restless nights and unfocused days.

The distance between my dorm and my university department could be walked in about ten minutes through the beautiful campus, which looked even more appealing decorated with October foliage. Attending an early-morning class made me slowly follow the familiar path without much thought. Since it was around the time birds awoke, only unfortunate students with early classes like myself wandered the cobblestone walkway. As I approached my destination, I suddenly saw a very brief scene in my mind's eye. I am not sure if it was a vision or a daydream, but it was as vivid as the concrete building towering in front of me.

My vision's setting was also outdoors, but it was somewhere else. There was a backdrop of snowy mountains and a blue, cloudless sky. It seemed like a spring day; the atmosphere was fresher and more alive than the fall air I was breathing. The only person in the scene was a little girl sitting on the grass, seemingly preoccupied with the toys in front of her. She did not appear to be an important character, as she was tiny compared with the mountains and the meadow leading up to them. The girl had long, dark hair like mine and was wearing a simple white dress. Suddenly, two giant hands came down from the heavens and offered the busy girl a present. The owner of the hands was so big that I could not see him; I saw only his hands. The present he held down to the little girl was beautiful beyond description. It was wrapped exquisitely and glowed so brightly that it was almost too much to look at. In an instant, I knew that this gift was something beyond any mortal's imagination and was much more valuable and important than anything man could possess. After a while, the little girl looked up and saw the dazzling gift that had come down from the skies. She thought for a moment, then said: "No, thank you; I have these toys to play with."

"Unbelievable!" I thought. "Silly little girl!" I wanted to say. "How could you possibly compare your petty little toys with that gift? How could you refuse such a splendid present? Do you not see that your life will be changed forever?" I felt like reaching into the vision and slapping some sense into that clueless child. But soon after these questions erupted in my mind, I realized that the little girl was none other than myself. I was the one who was utterly preoccupied with life's little worries, not seeing the big picture and thinking that what I saw in front of me was all that there ever could be. I was the one who took forever to notice that somebody had been trying to get my attention for a very long time. I was the one who was afraid to lose her career and her friends, which were pathetic little possessions in comparison with what God was offering me. I was the one who had refused the Divine Gift.

All of this took place in a span of mere seconds. The Holy Spirit had given me a little shove at the crossroads, making it clear which path to take. Choosing the same path as that little girl meant a life of earthly security and comfort, but what was that compared with eternal life? In that moment, I decided to accept the magnificent gift and open it layer by layer for the rest of my life, trusting that one day I would see the owner of those hands face to face. This hope welled up so strongly in my soul that I did not care how narrow the gate was or how less traveled the road. Then and there, I picked up the plow again and started pushing, and this time I was not looking back.

∙ ∙ ∙

Lydia offered everything she owned to the service of the Lord. Once she encountered the gift of God through Paul's preaching, she received it and responded generously. Note also that her response was within her means, rooted in the life she already led. She did not look at Paul and his followers and think, "I want to be just like them, so I must travel the empire." Of course, some of us are called to be missionaries, to cross the seas and the deserts to bring the Good News of Christ to those who are ignorant of him, but most of us are called to serve where we are. Lydia's big house and her resources could be used for the growing Church, while her newly baptized household learned from those who were more mature in the Faith. Lydia became so prominent in the Church in Philippi that Saint Luke mentioned her by name more than once in the Acts of the Apostles (and he did not like naming names unless they were important).

Lydia accepted the surprise that the Lord put in front of her. It is not so hard to imagine the scenarios and the worries that may have clouded her mind as she made her decision. After all, the Roman Empire was not friendly to Christians just yet. But she accepted the gift and moved forward in order to support the kingdom of God to the best of her abilities and according to the gifts the Lord had given her.

At some point in our lives, the Lord knocks on our doors with a surprise. Often this surprise is not something we expected or wanted, but always it is something we need, not only for our own salvation, but also for our household's. What we do with his unexpected gift could be life changing — just as it was for Lydia.

Saint Lydia, pray for us so that we may recognize the great gift God offers us in himself and receive it with joy as you did.

QUESTIONS FOR REFLECTION

What inspires you the most in Lydia's story?

Can you recall a time when the Lord gave you a gift, a surprise? How did you respond? What would you change?

Lydia embraced her role in serving the Church and spreading the Gospel. What do you think your role is? How can you embrace it more fully, following Lydia's example?

12

Our Lady

HOW CAN YOU KEEP THE FIRE ALIVE?

Read John 2:1-10

Two little girls ran after a boy, who teased them with a cookie. Their curly hair bounced as they screamed in joy to get hold of the treat the mischievous boy managed to get his hands on. The joyful noise of the days-long wedding filled the air: people laughing, dancing, and asking for more food and more drink. Colorful fabrics and fresh flowers decorated the tables. The aroma of freshly baked bread and roast lamb hung in the air. Servers whizzed all around, filling the cups of the guests who celebrated the brand-new union by downing as much wine as possible. After all, it was a momentous day — a day of feasting, celebration, and dancing.

The little boy ran into a woman who was sitting at the lower end of the table. She caught him by the arm as he stumbled. The cookie flew into the air, and one of the girls caught it. With their prize in hand, the girls ran off, curls still bouncing.

The boy's cheeks turned red at his clumsiness, but the lady straightened his clothes and ruffled his hair. Her smile did not show any anger or disturbance, which filled his heart with serenity. He exhaled a sigh of relief. The lady's gentle smile reached her eyes, which were two brown oceans of warmth. The boy could not help but smile back. For a moment, he was filled with peace; then he resumed his chasing full force. The lady watched him run after the girls, crow's feet deepening around her eyes as she chuckled.

Then her eyes focused on the only troubled faces in this otherwise joyful evening. What could be wrong? The men around her continued their talk, as she left to inquire:

> On the third day there was a marriage at Cana in Galilee, and the mother of Jesus was there; Jesus also was invited to the marriage, with his disciples. When the wine failed, the mother of Jesus said to him, "They have no wine." (John 2:1–3)

Her Son had warm, deep eyes like hers, eyes that pierced into your soul. When he talked to his mother, a slight smile appeared on his face. Love for the woman who birthed and raised him poured out in his every gesture. She knew her Son and his mission on this earth well enough simply to state the fact of the matter. She did not demand or reprimand, but simply gazed at him with the same loving eyes that had just looked upon the little boy:

> And Jesus said to her, "O woman, what have you to do with me? My hour has not yet come." His mother said to the servants, "Do whatever he tells you." Now six stone jars were standing there, for the Jewish rites of purification, each holding twenty or thirty gallons. Jesus said to them, "Fill the jars with water." And they filled them up to the brim. He said to them, "Now draw some out, and take it to the steward of the feast." So they took it. When the steward of the feast tasted the water now become wine, and did not know where it came from (though the servants who had drawn the water knew), the steward of the feast called the bridegroom and said to him, "Every man serves the good wine first; and when men have drunk freely, then the poor wine; but you have kept the good wine until now." (John 2:1–10)

Venerable Mary of Agreda writes about this occasion in her work *Mystical City of God*:

> This answer of Christ was not intended as a reproach, but contained a mystery; for the most prudent Queen had not asked for a miracle by mere accident, but by divine light. She knew that the opportune time for the manifestation of the divine power of her Son was at hand. She, who was full of wisdom and knowledge concerning the works of the Redemption and was well informed at what time and on what occasions the Lord was to perform them; therefore, she could not be ignorant of the proper moment for the beginning of this public manifestation of Christ's power.

Our Mother Mary, who never left the side of her Son, knew much more than we give her credit for. Because she was a loved and cherished mother, her divine Son obliged her. What is remarkable in the manner of her asking is her resolute confidence in her Son and her relationship with him. Her maternal heart went out to a couple facing a most mundane situation during a wedding. Her love for the newlywed couple led people to Christ, because her love had burned like a quiet, eternal fire from her conception.

The fire Mary carried in her heart and soul helped her to navigate the stormy seas in her life on earth. It was not a roaring blaze that consumed everything on its path, but more like a perpetual flame that radiated the warmth of charity, hope, and faith to everyone who came near.

The angel Gabriel called her "full of grace," saying in essence, "I will show you reverence because you excel me in the fullness of grace." His reverence for the Blessed Mother did not stop there. The angel, who stood before the Lord and delivered his divine word, declared that the virgin was even more familiar with the Lord: "The Lord is with thee." This young Jewish girl would become the sacred temple of the Holy Spirit, the new Ark of the Covenant. Who could claim to be closer to God? Saint Thomas Aquinas tells us:

> Therefore she was immune to every curse, and thereby blessed amongst women, for she alone put away the curse and carried the blessing, and the door of paradise opened; therefore the name Mary becomes her, which is interpreted Star of the Sea, because just as sailors are directed to port by the star of the sea, so Christians are directed by Mary to glory.†

---

† "Saint Thomas Aquinas on the Hail Mary," *Catholic Dossier* (May–June 1996), posted on EWTN, accessed November 11, 2020, https://www.ewtn.com/catholicism/library/saint-thomas-aquinas-on-the-hail-mary-5884.

Eve sought a fruit that would not give her what she wanted. The forbidden fruit did not make her a god; instead, her disobedience stripped her of whatever closeness to divinity she had enjoyed. But the Lord would give mankind yet another fruit: "Blessed is the fruit of thy womb." What Eve could not find in the fruit she took from the forbidden tree, the Blessed Virgin found in the fruit of her womb, for through Christ we are united with God and became partakers in his divinity. Thus, Saint Thomas writes, "Eve could not find in her fruit what no sinner can find in his sin. Therefore, what we desire, we should seek in the fruit of the Virgin. Here is a fruit blessed by God, because he has so filled him with every grace that it comes to us by showing him reverence."‡

Our Blessed Mother guides us in the dark toward the fruit of her womb. Not only is she our role model in womanhood and motherhood, but she holds our hands so that we don't fall off the cliff in the toil of this world. She is always willing to share that perpetual flame of her heart. Like a loving mother, she will not refuse to help us, because her only mission is to lead lost souls to her Son.

Our Lady's humility and perseverance should inspire every Catholic, but especially those of us who struggle with accepting the little paths to holiness that the Lord calls us to follow. It is said that the devil is more afraid of Mary than anything else, because her humility is something he cannot replicate. We, as her daughters, are left with two choices at the end of the day: Are we going to do whatever Jesus tells us, or are we going to follow our own wills?

· · ·

The past is a funny thing. Our wounds cling to our memories

---
‡ Ibid.

like little leeches that drain grace and joy. We forget a beloved friend's birthday, but we remember in vivid detail an offense that happened twenty years ago. My motherland is surely full of unpleasant memories for me, but there are also many good ones if I choose to dwell on the light instead of the darkness.

Mary was for a long time a blind spot in my Christian life, because I refused to see the good in my past. Intellectually, I had no problem with any of the Church's Marian doctrines. If anything, the fact that the Catholic Church held a woman in such high esteem, calling her the Mediatrix, the Mother of God, the Ark of the Covenant, and the Queen of Angels, hammered into me the truth that man and woman were both created in God's image and then redeemed by the same Savior. There are no second-class citizens in the kingdom of God.

All was good in my head, nicely organized in the cabinet labeled "Mary" and safely shut away. In reality, however, I had no idea how to relate with the Mother of all sinners. What would she tell me if she knew what a failure I was as a mother and a wife? Would she be mad if I told her I forgot to pray the Rosary again? Would she tell me that the gates of heaven are closed to me? She is, after all, the Queen of Heaven.

When I became a mother, I finally understood the love Mother Mary must feel for us, because the Lord put the spark of that perpetual flame in the heart of every woman, whether she becomes a biological mother or not. That wall of ice started to melt slowly when my kids took their first steps or gave me that first awkward kiss. It melted even more every time I said a Hail Mary for them when they woke up after a nightmare. In time, the furrowed eyebrows Mary had in my imagination gave way to the tender, loving eyes of Our Lady, who points to her own pierced heart. I need not worry about being perfect before I run to her. She takes me as I am and wants to guide me to holiness, making the spark a little brighter each day.

For me, the turning point was becoming a mother, because my heart was hardened. I remember looking at Rock the first night we brought him home. He was fussing in his crib without being able to roll, move, or even control his hands. His survival was utterly and completely dependent on his parents. The Lord had granted me an overwhelming power over this tiny person. What would I do with it?

Oh, how astounding that motherly love was! Frustrating often, yes, but then unbelievably vast. My love for my husband is conditional in a way, as I expect some reciprocity. But my love for my children is as close as I can get to unconditional love. If, in my sinful heart, where resentment and laziness often linger, I can still feel such an emotion, how much more, then, must God love us! How much more did Mary love Jesus and, by extension, everyone he died for! Confronted with the beauty of love, I found many a missed grace in my past.

In the television show *Doctor Who*, there is an alien species, the Ood, part of whose brain is external. This tennis ball–size part of the brain is attached to the rest of the brain by something like an umbilical cord. The Ood have to carry around that small part of their brain in their hands, utterly vulnerable to anyone who intends to hurt them. When I had children, and the fog of the newborn phase disappeared, I realized that I had become an Ood. Every time I had a baby, someone took a piece of my heart and gave it to the baby. I loved those babies more than I loved myself, but at times I was utterly helpless to help them. If they were sick, I wished I could feel the pain and the discomfort instead of them. They carried a piece of my heart with them. I had never been that vulnerable in my life, and again, this is a person feeling indescribable love despite her sinfulness and selfishness. Motherhood had turned that spark into a tiny flame.

One of my favorite icons of Mary is titled Our Lady of Perpetual Help. Mary, in a dark-red dress and with a solemn face, holds her Son. Angels offer him instruments of his coming Passion. The frightened Christ Child has run to his mommy for consolation, and one of his sandals has come off in his haste. If the Second Person of the Trinity ran to Mary in a time of distress, then we, too, can run to her — to the woman who carried and gave birth to the Word Incarnate, whose heart was pierced when he died, and who was assumed into heaven. Mary, the Mother of God, has become the first person I turn to at the beginning of each day, very much as my own children seek me as soon as they open their eyes. Like the frightened Christ Child whose first instinct was to run to his mommy, I learned to find comfort in her arms.

In return, she has been teaching me how to make tiny good habits part of my life so that the tiny flame can be fed daily, and one day turn into fire. These tiny habits include smiling at my children even when I do not want to, serving without complaint, trying to find the good in a person I strongly dislike, not taking offense when my husband forgets or neglects something I asked, and turning my eyes away from myself. In all these small and simple things, she holds our hands every day, like the little toddlers that we are, and walks us to her Divine Son, always repeating her last recorded words: "Do whatever he tells you." After all, she was the one who was present at the Incarnation, when the Son of God was born, when he performed his first miracle, when he was crucified, and when the Holy Spirit came down. I once heard a priest say that Mary wasn't at the tomb on Easter Sunday with the other women, because the first thing the Risen Christ did was run to his mother, just as he always did.

If we want to keep the fire of our faith alive in the daily grind of womanhood, there are two things we should do: run to Mary and form tiny good habits. Mother Church, in her divinely guided wisdom, gave us a tiny tool to form a tiny habit that involves Mary: praying the Hail Mary. It is only fitting to end a book about becoming a daughter, a wife, and a mother by delving a little more deeply into the Church's perennial appeal to the Mother of God.

This world is broken, and every minute we spend brooding on the past is a minute that is stolen from the service of the Lord. Through his death and resurrection, the Son of God, the Word Incarnate, gave us the grace to rise above pain and above any hurts from our past, if only we let him squeeze out of our souls the taint of our own sin and the sins of others.

When worries, darkness, and sin close in from all sides, remember the wedding at Cana and do what the Mother of God told the servants: "Do whatever he tells you."

QUESTIONS FOR REFLECTION

What image does the account of the wedding at Cana create in your mind? How does this affect your perception of Mary?

Do you find it easy to relate to Our Lady?

What tiny habits can you form in your life to keep the fire alive? How can you ask Mary to help you with this each day?

Epilogue

"Saint Anthony, please, help me find my zombie," prayed my seven-year-old as he walked around the house looking for the green plastic figure. My kids play video games, watch TV, and eat sand whenever they can. There is more than enough potty humor; our chicken nugget and peanut butter consumption would be frowned upon by many health-conscious moms I know; the odd-sock basket has overtaken the laundry room; and for some reason there are goldfish crackers everywhere. But then there are those moments when Rock asks for Saint Anthony's help, Love sings the Gloria perfectly during Mass, and King tells me, "Jesus loves you, Mommy." Things are imperfect in this messy house of ours, but life is good.

Not easy, but good.

A reluctance to surrender overshadowed my womanhood for a long time. These were uncharted waters for me, especially because I did not have faithfully Catholic wives and mothers around me to show me the way. But slowly, that reluctance turned into confidence, not in myself, but in the Lord, who is still patiently squeezing the yucky stuff out of this woman. There is still a long way to go before I become a delectable sausage, but by the grace of God, every day I grow closer.

I'd like to offer one last picture of a woman in the New Testament. This depiction of a Mary — usually thought to be Mary Magdalene — was the one I most identified with when I became a Christian:

> And behold, a woman of the city, who was a sinner, when she learned that he was at table in the Pharisee's house, brought an alabaster flask of ointment, and standing behind him at his feet, weeping, she began to wet his feet with her tears, and wiped them with the hair of her head, and kissed his feet, and anointed them with the ointment. (Luke 7:37–38)

Jesus had saved me from a sinful life, but in my naivete, I thought that one day of devotion, as beautiful as it was, would carry me through the storms of life. It would take the life of a wife and a mother for me to learn that the Lord had given me his peace and I was to live my life in his shadow, constantly anointing and wiping his feet. Not one time, but often, every day, and with every breath. When I lose sight of that hope and peace, life's worries cloud my day, and my joy disappears. As his daughters, as wives to his sons, and as mothers to his children, we need to remember:

> *And he said to the woman, "Your faith has saved you; go in peace." (Luke 7:50)*

About the Author

Derya M. Little has a Ph.D. in politics from Durham University, England, and an M.A. in history from Bilkent University, Turkey. She is the author of several books, including *From Islam to Christ: One Woman's Path through the Riddles of God* (2017), *A Beginner's Guide to the Latin Mass* (2019), and the young-adult fiction series *Two Fallen Worlds: Lost* and *Found* (2018). She lives in a small town with her husband and their five children. She can be visited online at DeryaLittle.com.